PRODUCTION LINE TO FRONTLINE

BOEING

B-17
FLYING
FORTRESS

SERIES EDITOR: TONY HOLMES

PRODUCTION LINE TO FRONTLINE • 2

BOEING
B-17 FLYING FORTRESS

Michael O'Leary

OSPREY
AVIATION

FRONT COVER A veritable sea of shiny B-17G Flying Fortress nose sections head toward mating with wings and rear fuselages, whilst a near-complete aircraft receives the finishing touches in the foreground

BACK COVER Boeing workers celebrate the completion of yet another B-17G during 1944

TITLE PAGE Classic Erik Miller photograph of a buxom Vega worker atop a Cheyenne tail turret

First published in Great Britain in 1998 by Osprey Publishing

Elms Court, Chapel Way, Botley, Oxford, OX2 9LP, United Kingdom

© 1998 Osprey Publishing Limited

ISBN 1 85532 814 3

Edited by Tony Holmes
Page design by Tony Truscott
Cutaway Drawing by Mike Badrocke

Origination by Appletone Graphics, Bournemouth
Printed through Worldprint Ltd, Hong Kong

98 99 00 01 02   10 9 8 7 6 5 4 3 2 1

EDITOR'S NOTE
To make this new series as authoritative as possible, the editor would be extremely interested in hearing from any individual who may have relevant photographs, documentation or first-hand experiences relating to the elite pilots, and their aircraft, of the various theatres of war. Any material used will be fully credited to its original source. Please write to Tony Holmes at 10 Prospect Road, Sevenoaks, Kent, TN13 3UA, Great Britain.

FOR A FREE CATALOGUE OF ALL BOOKS PUBLISHED BY OSPREY PLEASE WRITE TO:
The Marketing Manager, Osprey Publishing Limited, PO Box 140, Wellingborough, Northants, NN8 4ZA

CONTENTS

INTRODUCTION

WELCOME TO THE SECOND BOOK in Osprey's *Production Line to Frontline* series. As with the first volume on the North American Aviation P-51 Mustang, we have attempted to place the design of the aircraft within the time period of its creation and greatest operational usage. So, although the B-17 Flying Fortress soldiered on in various roles after the conclusion of World War 2, we have stopped our coverage of the famed bomber at the end of that conflict.

Few aircraft have endured such a stop-and-start development as the Flying Fortress. From a prototype developed with company funds, the design would have to go through numerous business, political, and military upheavals before its future was even partially secured. Also, the aircraft would experience myriad design changes prior to it really living up to its name.

Always hampered by the original limited bomb load specification, the B-17 was nearly eliminated by the inferior Douglas B-18 Bolo, itself a derivation of the DC-2 commercial transport. Fortunately, America obtained a small force of early B-17s and the type soon gained international fame through both Boeing's and the Army Air Corps' (AAC) clever use of publicity.

One of America's true production line success stories was the creation of the BVD (Boeing, Vega, Douglas) Pool that saw a steady stream of bombers pouring out of the assembly hangars of three major aeronautical concerns. BVD also proved that such co-ordinated production could be undertaken with an absolute minimum of problems – Vega proved to be a particularly shining example, delivering their first Flying Fortress six months ahead of the military's schedule, and one month ahead of the company's own internal schedule.

It must be remembered that this production effort was accomplished by average men and women from all across American who, in a country still gripped by the effects of the Great Depression, headed to the factories to find employment. The majority of these employees were completely uneducated when it came to matters aeronautical, but intensive training courses soon found ex-farm workers and house wives turning out advanced military aircraft that proved to be second to none.

As with the first volume in this series, we have endeavoured to find fresh photographs to illustrate all aspects of the B-17 from 'production line to frontline'. The pre-war years of B-17 operations were poorly recorded on film, and of those photographs that were taken, many have been lost to the ravages of time. However, we hope that the production line photographs – many of which have never been seen – well illustrate the national effort that went into building the Fortress, with a particular focus on the vast utilisation of women on the production line.

I would like to take this opportunity to thank Scott Bloom for the provision of the vintage B-17 advertisements, and Boeing Historic Archive for a number of the photos included within this volume.

As always, we appreciate reader input on this and future volumes in the series, and the author would be pleased to receive further information, photographs and suggestion at PO Box 6490, Woodland Hills, California, USA, 91365.

Michael O'Leary
Los Angeles November 1998

CHAPTER 1

THE PROTOTYPE

THE DATE OF MAY 1934 should be considered a watershed mark in the development of American military airpower. During that month, the Army Air Corps (AAC) issued a specification for a new 'multi-engined' bomber. The specification was available to all interested aeronautical concerns, but it should be noted during this time period 'multi-engined' was usually considered to mean two engines. During 1934, most aircraft builders were just struggling along – the effects of the Great Depression still lay heavy upon American industry in general, and the aeronautical industry in particular.

Boeing had also been experiencing plenty of other problems aside from those associated with the Depression. The company had originally part of a large organisation by the name of United Aircraft, which included not only Boeing, but an airline of the same name as the parent company, an engine company, and various airframe component companies. When United Airlines placed an order for 60 of Boeing's new Model 247 twin-engined airliners, the US government cried halt, claiming the company had become a monopoly – something the government viewed as a serious threat to free trade. The government started legal action against United Aircraft, and made sure Boeing would not have a ready-made market for their aircraft.

Thus, the early 1930s were looking even blacker for the airframe company. However, Boeing had plenty of talent amongst its modest workforce, and management and the company's aeronautical engineers knew that they could produce superior aircraft if just given the chance. The Model 247 airliner had proven to be a rugged, well-built, machine which was useful for short and secondary routes, but Douglas, with its DC-2 and magnificent DC-3, had all but destroyed the 247's market.

Even though the decade comprising the 1930s saw the industrialised world gripped by the effects of the Great Depression, the period also inspired one of the most distinctive design forms of the 20th century. The style, known variously as 'streamline', 'moderne' or the more formal 'Art Deco', filled the decade with sleek and elegant shapes that ranged from streamlined toasters to the towering skyscrapers that thrust their pointed towers higher and higher into the skies above American cities. However, one of the design forms that lent itself best to the designer's lust for streamlined, clean and efficient shapes was that of the aircraft.

Military aviation was also undergoing a revolution at this time as 'clunky' biplanes were being replaced by gleaming monoplanes with higher speeds, greater range and a variety of deadly armaments. Since the effects of Art Deco (a popularised term for the 1925 *Exposition Internationale des Arts Decoratifs et Industriels Modernes*, which was held in Paris and revolutionised the design world with the many geometric and streamlined items on display) were sweeping across the implements of society, it was not unnatural that the world of military aviation would also be deeply, and permanently, changed.

Boeing was a believer in solidly built all-metal monoplanes. The 247, the Model 200 Monomail, and the experimental YB-9 bomber had all proven that the company's designs were strong, efficient and high-performing. Still, developing advanced aircraft without government backing was a very risky and costly business, but in early 1934 Boeing managed to secure a development contract for wind tunnel testing and technical development of an experimental long-range bomber initially designated XBLR-1. Boeing deluged the AAC with piles of data

Sleek, elegant and in stark contrast to the vintage Fords in the employees' parking lot, the completed Model 299 is pushed out by manpower for its first engine runs

for a new 'sky giant' with a wingspan of nearly 150 ft. The AAC liked the idea for the new aircraft, which the company duly designated the Model 294 and the military the XB-15 in July 1936.

However, the XB-15 was not going to be an easy aircraft to design and construct, and work quickly began to bog down as many detail problems had to be resolved. At the same time construction of the 247 and Boeing fighters such as the P-26 Peashooter was rapidly dropping off, and something had to be done to keep the company in the black. Thus, the AAC specification of May 1934 was a virtual godsend.

Boeing management and engineering staff realised that the term 'multi-engined' really meant that the AAC wanted a new twin-engined aircraft with which to eventually replace the Martin B-10, then in frontline service. At the heart of the request for a new bomber was the aircraft's ability to carry a two-ton bomb load for 1000 miles. Fully aware that other aircraft companies were also developing twin-engined designs for the competition (these machines would all have basically similar capabilities and performance), Boeing knew that their design had to be fairly radical and boast better performance than its competitors.

The Boeing team, headed by Claire Egtvedt, reasoned that in order to achieve high performance, more engines were needed. In the past, extra engines had been added to designs (especially the tri-motors, which had proven popular in the late 1920s and early 1930s) just so the weight hauled into the air could be increased. The extra engines rarely did anything to increase overall performance and, in fact, they usually did just

With the turret positions cloaked in canvas, the Model 299's fuselage poses for a portrait on 2 July 1935. The hand-crafted prototype displays the excellent workmanship that distinguished Boeing aircraft of the period

the opposite – especially in case of engine failure. Egtvedt reasoned an airframe which combined the construction techniques of the Model 247 airliner and the overall configuration of the uncompleted XB-15 would offer superior performance over any twin-engined design then on the drawing boards. Giff Emery was assigned as project engineer, with Edward C Wells (then only 24) as assistant project engineer.

The AAC further defined its proposal during August 1934, the requirement now including a top speed of 250 mph at 10,000 ft, a useful load (a rather purposely ambiguous statement) to be carried at the same altitude with a cruise speed of 220 mph and an endurance of ten hours. Further demands on the new design stated that the machine should also be able to achieve an altitude of 10,000 ft in five minutes, while an altitude of 7000 ft should be maintained with one engine out while carrying the 'useful load'.

Boeing had already started design work on its bomber when carefully worded questions to the AAC found that they had no major objection to a four-engined design. Given the Boeing designation of Model 299, work on the prototype was authorised on 26 September 1934 and construction began with initial company-supplied funding of $275,000, although this

Employees and spectators get a chance to view Boeing's newest creation shortly after the Model 299's roll out. Note the gleaming polished aluminium finish and the awkward gun cupola in the nose

amount would nearly double before the final product got into the air.

For power, the engineering team had settled on the Hornet radial built by Pratt & Whitney. A rugged engine capable of developing a maximum of 750 hp, the R-1690E Hornet was a known quantity, and not an experimental unit which would cause the company more worry. Taking the lead from the 247 and XB-15 designs, the Model 299's wing utilised tubular strutting to produce a structure of extreme strength. The engines were mounted in front of streamlined nacelles which connected large fuel tanks, whilst the fuselage was also a masterpiece of Art Deco streamlining, being almost airfoil-like in shape. An elegant 'shark fin' vertical tail topped the extremely pointed rear fuselage section.

Defensive positions were also enclosed in sleek streamlined cupolas on the sides of the fuselage and at the rear portion of the humped crew compartment. A further defensive position was installed in the nose and consisted of a blister, which could be turned 360° to increase the field of fire for the single weapon. All guns could be either .30 or .50-cal Brownings.

The interior of the Model 299 was almost as shiny as the outside, since the natural alclad finish was left devoid of the zinc chromate green paint synonymous with the interiors of American combat aircraft. This photograph, taken on 18 June 1935, shows the complex right side blister, and its .30-cal weapon, in the stowed position. The machine gun was fitted with one ammunition tray, while two others are seen in their mountings on the side of the fuselage

The Model 299 incorporated many of the concepts of the Model 294, which had not flown by the time the first Flying Fortress took to the skies. The Army Air Corps issued a specification for a 'Long Range Airplane Suitable for Military Purposes' on 14 April 1934, and Boeing's proposal duly won the contract, with the new aircraft being originally designated XBLR-1 – this was soon changed to XB-15, however. The bomber was the heaviest and largest aircraft built in the USA up to that point, and was fitted with two main landing gear wheels on each side to support the weight. Originally designed to utilise four Allison V-3420 powerplants, the aircraft was actually fitted with four Pratt & Whitney R-1830 radials of just 1000 hp each, making the bomber distinctly under-powered. However, even in this condition, the XB-15 did manage to set several payload records. Despite this, the aircraft was destined to remain a prototype, failing to see operational use as a bomber and instead being converted into a cargo hauler with the new designation XC-105. After years of faithful service, the XB-15, which had made its first flight on 15 October 1937, was scrapped shortly before war's end at Kelly Field, in Texas

The bombardier's sighting panel was installed in a nook under the fuselage directly behind the nose, which resulted in a modest fuselage kink that slightly marred the Model 299's streamlining. Crew positions were unusually comfortable for the day, with the two pilots enjoying fairly good visibility from a cockpit full of all the appropriate period 'bells and whistles'. Since time was extremely important, Boeing workers forged ahead with complete dedication, realising that success for the 299 meant a continuation of their employment.

The sleek aircraft, its aluminium skin polished until it glowed, was rolled out of the factory on 17 July 1935 before an admiring throng of employees and pressmen. The new aircraft really did not look like anything which had come before, its lines giving it an almost spaceship-like appearance and, from that moment on, the American press and public alike began a love affair with the bomber which has lasted through to this day. Press reports enthused on the bomb bay, which could carry up to 4800 lbs of bombs in vertical stacks. The five machine guns, and their defensive field of fire, were also much com-

The rather spartan cockpit of the Model 299, complete with two wooden control wheels, was photographed on 25 July 1935. Boeing's name plate was fitted to the throttle quadrant, and reads 1 July 1935 as the date of manufacture

mented upon, leading *Seattle Times* reporter Dick Williams to write of the aircraft as a 'flying fortress'. Boeing liked the sobriquet, capitalised the two 'fs' and then registered the name 'Flying Fortress' as a company trademark.

After thorough engine checks, systems tests and ground handling runs, the Model 299 was taken aloft for the first time on 28 July by company pilot Leslie Tower. The big aircraft handled quite well, but problems were experienced with tail wheel shimmy. The time schedule was tight, and every effort was made to get the bomber to Wright Field, in Ohio, for the competition. Although the Model 299 carried full AAC markings, it was a company-owned, civilian registered, aircraft which wore the registration X13372 in the standard positions on the wings and rudder.

Boeing's major competitors for the AAC contract were the Douglas DB-1 and Martin 146, priced respectively at $99,150 and $85,910 apiece for a small production run – the Boeing product would cost a staggering $196,730 per unit for the same production run! The Model 299 had enemies from the start as some AAC officers reasoned that the service should not be equipped with anything beyond a speedy twin-engined medium bomber, letting the aircraft's speed replace defensive armament. Also, more twin-engined bombers could be purchased with the limited available funding. A few of these officers even went as far as to publicly express the thought that army pilots would not be able to handle the big bomber because it was too complex!

In order to get the aircraft to Ohio, seven test flights (accumulating approximately 14 hours of flying time) were undertaken over a three-week period, and Boeing employees worked overtime to rectify every fault or problem – by that stage the company's work force numbered just 600 employees, compared to a previous high of 1700. The gleaming Model 299 made its run from Boeing Field to Wright Field on 20 August, managing to achieve an average speed of 233 mph while covering the distance in nine hours and three minutes.

At Wright Field, evaluation of the three aircraft began in earnest, and although the Model 299 proved to be faster than both the Martin and Douglas designs, its speeds were not as high as had been hoped for by Boeing. The company had made a major investment of funds to reach this stage of the competition, and the fate of the organisation hung on the AAC decision. In all aspects of testing (range, speed, payload and firepower), the 299 was proving superior to the other aircraft, but then on 30 October, disaster struck.

Early in the morning, mechanics ran up the Hornets and made some adjustments to the carburettors on engines three and four. However, when the flight crew arrived they wanted to get airborne as soon as possible and the cowlings were fitted back to the engines without the same adjustments having been made to the carburettor jets on engines' one and two. The flight crew consisted of Maj P P Hill, chief of the flying branch at Wright Field, Lt Donald L Putt, chief pilot for Boeing Leslie Tower, test observer John Cutting and Wright Field employee Mark Koegler.

The mission for the day was to obtain the first climb to approximately 20,000 ft at predetermined indicated climbing speeds, as required in Expenditure Order No 3743-10 (dated 7 October 1935) issued from the office of the Chief Engineer. It was intended to obtain the rate of climb at sea level, time to climb to 10,000 ft and the service ceiling from the results of this flight.

The engines were started, but according to some witnesses, there seemed to be a considerable delay before the bomber began to taxy at approximately 0900. As there was no paved runway at Wright Field at this time, Maj Hill simply turned the aircraft into the prevailing wind, locked the tail wheel and proceeded to do his engine power and magneto checks. A few seconds after 0909, with everything still seemingly okay, the pilot advanced the throttles and started the take-off roll across the grass field. As it gathered speed, Lt Donald Putt later commented that he 'noticed it had a little tendency to weave. Maj Hill reached up once to adjust the throttles. As the plane tended to swing off to the left he opened the throttles a little on the left side'. After running on the ground for 15 to 17 seconds, the 299 lifted off in a little more than 1000 ft.

Soon after the aircraft left the ground, it seemed to some observers to enter a fairly acute rate of climb. Ed Wells commented 'the airplane seemed to steadily increase its angle of attack'. Other pilots on the ground estimated the angle of attack at approximately 45°. At this point, testimony became a bit confusing, and some witnesses felt that the two left motors cut out. This led the aircraft to yaw into the dead engines and the left wing dropped and the aircraft fell into a spin, apparently nearly completing 180°. The aircraft was apparently at an altitude of only 300 ft when this happened, and although it appears that the left wing did subsequently achieve a little more lift, it was that flying surface which first made contact with the ground, causing the aircraft to partially cartwheel before coming to rest upright and on fire.

Mark Koegler would recall, 'just at that instant we struck and the radio compartment simply burst into a mass of flames. Of course, I made an attempt to get out at the rear door of the radio compartment. I attempted three or four times to open the door and I couldn't do it. Finally, I just reared back and caved the door in. I felt the door let go, and I passed out then. I don't remember getting out of the ship. The next thing I knew I was lying on the ground and when I came to I raised up and saw the whole ship was afire'.

John Cutting would later testify, 'I went out the same exit as Lt Putt did. It was on the right side of the fuselage. At first I thought the fuselage had split open, but on checking up I found it had not. I saw Lt Putt clear away something and climb out and I immediately followed him'.

Koegler, Cutting and Putt escaped the Model 299 with varying degrees of injury and burns. However, Hill and Tower were trapped in the demolished cockpit as the fire increased. The accident had, of course, captured the attention of everyone on the field. 1Lt Robert K Giovannoli stated, 'I was standing there in front of the Operations building at the time it hit. The fire truck started out and at the time I didn't feel like there was anything I could do. I didn't immediately rush out, and I began to see them running out with fire extinguishers, and I got my car and picked up a few of the fire extinguishers, drove out and stood around for awhile. Before I started out I saw someone running around the crash and I was trying to find out how many had gotten out'.

As Lt Giovannoli and others got to the burning wreck, they saw Leslie Tower trying to get out of the cockpit through the front window on the co-pilot's side, and they ran to help him, pulling the gravely injured pilot from the window. At this point, Giovannoli, at great personal risk, entered the wreckage. 'Maj Hill raised up. We saw him and I climbed in the window and tried to help him out. Found that his foot was caught on the rudder. So we worried around him until we got that loose, then got him out, and then I left the scene of the accident'.

1Lt Leonard F Harmon recalled, 'I ran around the right wing and the next thing that I was aware of was that somebody had yelled. Giovannoli had started into the airplane. I ran around the nose of the ship and saw Maj Hill apparently raise up in the seat'.

The Model 299 with two earlier Boeing products, namely Model 248 fighters. The latter aircraft again showed the creativity of Boeing's engineering department by blending the company's design philosophy with the AAC's operational requirements. Using their own funds, as with the Model 299, Boeing completed and flew the new fighter (which received the designation XP-936) on 20 March 1932. The AAC was very pleased with the aircraft's performance and duly placed an order for 136 examples under the designation P-26. When flying at maximum speed, the Model 299 was exactly one mile per hour faster than the P-26

For his actions that day, Lt Giovannoli was to be awarded the Soldier's Medal, which was the highest decoration for bravery a member of the armed forces could receive for an act of heroism not directly involving action with an enemy. The citation for the award read;

'That 1st Lieut Robert K Giovannoli, Air Corps, did at Wright Field, on 30 October 1935, about 9:15 am, distinguish himself by displaying most unusual acts of heroism and self-sacrifice over and beyond the call of duty during the rescue of personnel of the Boeing Bombardment Airplane which crashed that date at Wright Field, Dayton, Ohio; in the way that he forced his way into the fuselage of the burning airplane and partially in order to extricate Mr Leslie R Tower (now deceased); that he then entered the burning compartment where he remained from six to eight minutes extricating, from an entrapped position, and passing through the window Major Ployer P Hill, Air Corps (now deceased), the Pilot and last occupant of the crashed airplane; that during the period he was within the fuselage where the fire was most intense, his own life being constantly in peril due to flames, smoke and fuel tank explosions; that he was directly responsible for the removal, alive, of Mr Leslie R. Tower and Major Ployer P Hill; that he was seriously injured and burned as a result of his voluntary action, the omission of which would not have justly subjected him to

The flying career of the Model 299 was to be quite short a one. This 30 October 1935 photograph shows the aircraft burning after crashing on take-off at Wright Field. Maj Ployer Hill was in the left seat and Boeing test pilot Leslie Tower in the right. Rescuers managed to pull both men from the shattered cockpit but Hill died soon after and Tower painfully lingered for a month before succumbing to extensive burns

any censure for shortcoming or failure in the performance of duty.'

In addition, he was recommended for and was to receive the Chaney Award for the year 1935. Sadly, 1Lt Robert Giovannoli was killed in a flying accident at Wright Field on 8 March 1936 before he could receive his highly deserved recognition.

So what happened to the Model 299? After a lengthy investigation, a safety board ruled that the aircraft had taken off with the control locks still in place, resulting in an uncontrollable aircraft. However, recent research indicates that this decision may have been more of a matter of immediacy rather than actual fact. Leaving the control locks in place was a failure of the crew rather than the aircraft. What if the steep rate of climb had caused the fuel flow to the engines to cut out due to a design or mechanical failure? This would have reflected poorly on the already controversial Model 299, and may not have resulted in further orders. What did cause the engines to cut out? It was never properly explained.

As it was, Boeing did not have a back up aircraft to take the stricken Model 299's place, and since the competition had not been finished, the Boeing design was basically out of the running and Douglas won with its DB-1.

The Model 299 cost $432,034 to build, and this almost completely exhausted the cash reserves of Boeing. The rear fuselage of the Model 299 was retained at Wright Field for testing of the side gun blisters and other gun mounts. However, the final chapter on the aircraft that had become known as the Flying Fortress was far from being written.

The shattered remains of the Model 299 shortly after the fire had been extinguished. Oddly, the relatively undamaged rear fuselage (note the open entrance door) was hauled back to the base, cleaned up, and used in later years as a testing device for B-17 armament, mounting various weapons and turrets

CHAPTER 2 SHARK FINS

THE UNFORTUNATE DEMISE of the Model 299 firmed up two camps of thought on the new Boeing aircraft – those who disliked the concept felt the aircraft should be dropped in favour of more twin-engined bombers, whilst those who favoured the 299 considered the design's excellent performance figures recorded before the accident more than supported the success of the Flying Fortress.

Before the crash, the AAC was considering ordering up to 65 B-17s (as the design had now been designated). After the accident, more conservative figures prevailed, and the order was cut back to the traditional 13 test and development machines – Y1B-17s (the 'Y' stood for the test and evaluation role and the '1' indicated the programme was specially funded). The size of the contract (Army Contract W535-ac-8306), issued on 17 January 1936, was partially attributed to the state of the AAC's coffers, for 133 twin-engined Douglas B-18 Bolos had also been ordered (this was the redesignated DB-1 of the fly-off competition). For the time, these two contracts amounted to a huge outlay of federal money, causing concern amongst certain segments of the population who strongly felt that these substantial sums could have been better spent on social projects to help get the isolationist nation out of the Great Depression.

Boeing and Seattle, however, were more than pleased to receive the work. Even 13 aircraft meant a continued chance of corporate survival, and the exponents of strategic bombing knew they would at least have some working prototypes with which to test their theories.

To get the aircraft built as quickly as possible, the Y1B-17 (Model 299B) remained very similar to the prototype. The landing gear leg was modified in order to facilitate more rapid changing of the wheel and tyre assembly, the crew complement was reduced to six and defensive armament consisted of five .30-cal machine guns in various positions. In a major change, the Pratt & Whitney Hornet radials were dropped in favour of Wright R-1820-39 Cyclones, which developed an extra 100 hp per motor. Also, the Air Corps felt that this engine had greater growth potential.

Work at Seattle proceeded rapidly, and the first of the sleek Y1B-17s was ready for test flying on 2 December 1936 (the aircraft was finished in Boeing's World War 1 plant, pending completion of a new facility dedicated to Y1B-17 production, and had to be taken by barge to the eastern side of the field for assembly), when Maj John D Corkille took the bomber aloft for a successful 50-minute flight. In an effort to avoid any accidents similar to that which had claimed the prototype, the AAC despatched Capt Stanley Umstead from Wright Field to Boeing to test each aircraft as it came off the production line.

On 7 December, after completing the third test flight of the number one aircraft, Umstead brought the bomber in for a landing at Boeing Field but stomped too aggressively on the brakes and tipped the Y1B-17 onto its nose. It skidded along tail up for all of 80 yards, and although a considerable amount of damage was caused, the gear did not collapse, saving the crew from death or injury. S/n 36-149 had its tail gently lowered back onto the tarmac and was towed to the factory for repair, but the future of the entire programme was once again exposed to speculation.

Another investigation was started into the overall feasibility of the strategic bomber. Both sides argued long and loud, but the programme was allowed to continue with the stipulation that another accident would spell the end for the Y1B-17. Work continued on the remaining machines, including an example set aside for static testing. As production continued, further improvements were also introduced to the aircraft, including

Climbing out of Wright Field, a Y1B-17 is seen during a test and evaluation flight. Note the Wright Field arrow marking immediately behind the side blister position. Externally, the new aircraft was almost identical to the Model 299, although the newer design had had its powerplants changed from Hornets to Cyclones, with attendant modifications to the cowlings and nacelles

the fitting of rubber de-icer boots to the leading edge of the wing and the substitution of fabric for aluminium on the flaps.

The first of the new Y1B-17s was delivered to the AAC in January 1937 and the last in August, the aircraft then being assigned to the 2nd Bombardment Group's (BG) 20th, 49th, and 96th Bombardment Squadrons (BS) at historic Langley Field, in Virginia. The group's experienced pilots and crews were given the task of wringing the big bomber out in order to discover whether there were any hidden flaws which would prevent the B-17 from becoming an effective combat tool.

Gen Frank Andrews, Commanding General Headquarters Air Corps, felt the Army's insistence on airpower playing merely a supporting role for ground battles was incorrect, and set about using the Y1B-17s as a showcase for developing theories of strategic bombing. Knowing the general public would be greatly impressed by the size and power of 'his' new aircraft, Andrews and his top officers instigated a plan to expose the bomber to as many citizens as possible.

Lt Col Robert C Olds, commander of the 2nd BG, fully approved of these publicity-fetching ideas, and briefed his men on how the success of strategic bombing as a whole depended entirely upon their success in promoting the bomber. In order

ABOVE Cockpit of a Y1B-17 (the aircraft were commonly referred to as YBs – even the nameplate in this photo reads YB-17), photographed on 31 October 1936. Comparison with the 299's cockpit is useful. Note the attractive laminated wood control wheels

RIGHT A Boeing engineer illustrates the use of the Y1B-17's belly gun position, with the .30 cal Browning at maximum rear deflection. As can be seen, visibility from this position was not all that great, but at least it did provide some form of protection – a feature lacking on most contemporary bombers. Note that the interior has been sprayed silver. This photograph was taken on 9 December 1938

to prevent a 299-style accident befalling his Y1B-17s, Olds drew up detailed pre-flight checks lists, since there were too many items in the aircraft to rely on memory alone – this was one of the first such examples of a now-standard item.

A perfect example of a typical 2nd BG operation was the 1938 Y1B-17 dash to South America, which saw the participating aircraft thoroughly groomed prior to departure. The trip was called a 'good-will tour', but in actuality, the mission was to show certain Nazi elements in that part of the world that America now possessed an aircraft that could cover long distances with an effective payload. Both Brazil and Argentina were visited, and the trip proved to be a great success – huge throngs of people swamped the 2nd's aircraft at each stop. Back home, the trip made daily headlines, and the public followed the route of the Flying Fortresses with interest.

A more effective display of the Y1B-17's capabilities saw the 2nd intercept the Italian ocean liner *Rex* some 700 miles from the American east coast. The mission was listed as a 'navigational exercise', but there is little doubt that its main point was to emphasise the fact that bombers could reach and destroy an incoming enemy fleet before it even posed a threat to the American mainland – Billy Mitchell had been right!

An image of what might have been. Numerous high-ranking Air Corps officers favoured the procurement of more twin-engined medium bombers, rather than putting all their funding into the purchase of a four-engined strategic bomber such as the B-17. The Douglas B-18 (numerous examples of which are seen at the Clover Field factory in Santa Monica on 26 August 1938) came close to completely replacing the B-17 in the military budget. Developed from the DC-2 transport, the aircraft was not an adequate weapon and did not see combat – except for coastal and anti-submarine patrol – during World War 2

YIB-17 on final to Langley. The 2nd BG's insignia has been painted on the forward nose, whilst the 'U.S. ARMY' titles under the wings were applied in Insignia Blue. Except for war games, the YIB-17s kept their natural metal finish. Note the fabric-covered flaps fully down

This intercept exercise did not fool top US Navy admirals, however, who were furious that the AAC would undertake such a mission over what they considered to be 'their territory'. This narrow, and stupid, thinking went as far as an attempt to have the AAC restricted to flights that did not exceed 100 miles from the American coastline! Fortunately, the attempt was not successful.

With the Flying Fortresses making almost daily headlines, the prestige of both the AAC and Boeing began to rise. The fledgling military service had suddenly gained a new stature and importance, and the aircraft was no longer regarded as just a frivolous toy.

The development of strategic tactical bombing was much discussed by the men of the 2nd BG. Eventually, they agreed bombing from high altitude would be ideal since this would place the aircraft at a safe distance from most anti-aircraft weapons, while enemy interceptors would have to strain to reach these rarefied heights. Accordingly, testing began with the Y1B-17s to see if the bombers could reach such altitudes, but when carrying a full load it was found that the engines would not develop enough power in the thin air.

While flight testing and development continued, an unusual incident befell Y1B-17 s/n 36-157 (the ninth example) whilst piloted by Lt William Bentley on 6 July 1937 which caused heavy damage to the aircraft. Lt Bentley made the following official report on 10 July;

'The following is a chronological report of the events during flight of Y1B-17 s/n 36-157 to Galax, Virginia, and return.

This Y1B-17 has been daubed with water-based camouflage for the 1938 war games. The AAC tried out a number of experimental paint schemes during the late 1930s but, for ease of maintenance, settled on Olive Drab and Neutral Grey immediately before the American entrance into World War 2. Over the correct terrain, the water-based paints could be very effective, rendering the bomber virtually invisible when viewed from above

'Airplane was given daily inspection by Tech Sgt John Mauro and crew prior to flight. All tanks were filled with gasoline, including bomb bay tanks, giving a total gas load on take-off of 2492 gallons.

'Crew consisted of eight. Estimated weight, including baggage and parachutes, etc, 2000 lbs. Estimated gross weight of airplane at time of accident, 41,592 lbs.

'Take-off at 1033 was normal, with a run of approximately 2500 ft. A climb of 600 ft per minute to 8000 ft was maintained with an airspeed (indicated) of 120 mph, then at approximately 400 fpm to 14,000 ft (15,000 actual).

'Ship was levelled off at 14,000 ft, and flight maintained at that altitude at 115-120 mph indicated (148-154 actual) to conduct gasoline consumption test. Autopilot was turned on at 1120 over Broadnax, Virginia, and engines were put in high blower. Engineering data was noted on engineering report at 1140, showing everything normal, with indicated airspeed of 120 mph. Last definite ground check, Danville, Virginia, on course.

'There was a more or less solid overcast below, the average ceiling of which was 13,000 ft with occasional breaks in which the ground was visible, and occasional piling up of clouds to 18,000 to 20,000 ft. The airplane passed through several of

This YIB-17 fuselage was photographed as during the bomber's construction on 16 March 1937. The YIBs were virtually all hand-finished machines

these clouds, the longest single period of which was less than ten minutes. On two instances, precipitation was seen, once as rain, and once as snow. In the first instance, a slight amount of ice formed on the antenna, the window eaves, the nose gun turret and the motor ring cowls. This ice dried or melted off a few moments later. Little ice was encountered in the manifolds. The airspeed was checked during this period, with heat on and off, to see if there was any ice forming, and no appreciable change was apparent. Snow was encountered once in brilliant sunshine, with no visible clouds above.

'At 1220, the airplane suddenly, with no warning whatsoever, did a snap half roll to the left and continued into a left spin. During the half roll, the pilot turned off the automatic pilot and took the controls. The wheel was in the full right position and the rudder in full right position, showing that the automatic pilot was endeavouring at the time to straighten out the airplane.

'The throttles were immediately closed, and after an estimated turn-and-a-half spin, level flight was resumed by utilising turn and bank indicator, airspeed, rate of climb and altimeter.

Boeing and the AAC took just about every possible opportunity to publicise the Y1B-17, as this photograph of a 2nd BG bomber over the Washington Monument in Washington, DC, proves

The gyro flight instrument was out, having hit the limiting pegs. Level flight was restarted at 11,000 ft and held for a few minutes until an open spot was encountered and, in this, the ship was tested for stability, flying qualities, etc. The airplane handled normally in every respect from 90 to 140 mph, and the gyro was found to function properly.'

After the crew got the aircraft back on the ground, the bomber was thoroughly inspected with the following observations noted;

'The wings of the airplane had undergone partial failure due to the buckling compression of the upper inter-spar corrugated sheet across its entire width close to Bulkhead No 14 in both the right and left wings. The damage was symmetrical with respect to the axis of the airplane, indicating that the two wings had sustained loads identical in direction and magnitude. As far as could be seen, no other principal structural elements were involved and the Engineering Section of the Division is now proceeding with an analysis of the damage with a view to making recommendations relative to measures necessary to permit delivery of the airplane by air to the factory.

'In the normal Y1B-17 airplane of 34,000 lbs, the allowable maximum severity of operation is represented by a pull-out of 3.67 G. This represents a total applied force of 3.67 x 34,000 = 125,000 lbs, which is therefore the maximum total force which this airplane is designed to withstand in service without permanent deformation. Consequently, the airplane when loaded to 41,500 lbs and subjected to an acceleration of approximately 4 G as shown by the V-G record (an on-board testing instrument being carried by the aircraft) was acted upon by a total force of 4 x 41,500 = 166,000 lbs. This exceeds the maximum allowable operating force by 166,000 - 125,000 = 41,000 lbs and, conse-

A basic B-17B fuselage in the assembly building, with the prototype Stratoliner vertical fin sticking up over the Fort's nose. This view shows to advantage how the top fuselage and gun cupolas were attached to the fuselage as separate units. The photograph was taken on 12 February 1939

quently, brings the loading well up into the range within which permanent distortion can be expected to take place. This range extends from the maximum allowable loading to the ultimate strength.

'In this case, the ultimate strength is the design weight (34,000 lbs) times the design load factor (5.5) = 187,000 lbs. The allowable being 125,000 lbs, gives a range of progressive failure of 187,000 - 125,000 = 62,000 lbs. Since the actual applied force was 166,000 lbs, the above range of 62,000 lbs was invalid to the extent of 41,000 lbs, or about 66 per cent. In other words, the load sustained by the airplane took up about two-thirds of the factor of safety provided for just such incidents.'

Lt Bentley and his passengers obviously had a lucky escape, but what had caused the incident? On 26 July the War Department issued a notice that stated;

'Experience in flying C-33, B-18 and B-17 types of airplanes equipped with automatic pilots has demonstrated that corrections made, when flying on the automatic pilot under conditions of side-slip or stall, may cause the airplane to spin.

This B-17B cockpit view shows both the new instrument arrangement and throttle installation. The control wheels are made of laminated wood, with brass tips. Note the huge Flying Fortress name plate just beneath the cockpit coaming behind the co-pilot's controls. The cockpit interior was sprayed zinc chromate, with various items picked out in black or grey. Finally, note the carpeting in front of the seats!

Automatic pilots should normally be disconnected and the airplane flown manually when flying in extremely turbulent air, atmospheric conditions in which the wing de-icers are operating, in climbs or straight away flight conditions near stalling speed of the airplane, and under conditions resulting from below standard power from one or more motors.'

At around the same time as this incident took place, the AAC decided to equip s/n 37-369 as a testbed for the development of General Electric (GE) turbo-superchargers, which were desperately needed to allow the bomber to attain the high altitudes stipulated in the combat doctrine created by the 2nd BG. This aircraft became the sole Y1B-17A, and various configurations were tested, including mounting the unit atop the forward nacelle, but eventually the best location was deemed to be at the bottom of the nacelle.

The aircraft made its first flight on 29 April 1938 and was delivered to the AAC for further testing on 31 January 1939. Basically the same as the earlier aircraft except for the addition of the turbo-superchargers, the Y1B-17A proved to be the answer for high-altitude bombing. With the turbo-superchargers engaged, the Wright R-1820-51 radials could develop 800 hp each at 25,000 ft, while the Y1B-17s' could only develop 775 hp at 14,000 ft, with the rating then falling off rapidly as the aircraft climbed above that level. Maximum speed for the Y1B-17A also increased to 295 mph at 25,000 ft, which was a figure that even the aircraft's critics had to admire.

The 2nd BG continued testing with their Y1B-17s at a fairly rapid pace, all the while taking note of what was going on in Europe. Oddly, neither Britain nor Germany, at that time, had an operational, modern, four-engined strategic bomber, instead relying on twin-engined 'mediums' as so favoured by many in the American military. Lightly armed and armoured, and not all that fast, these machines would suffer heavily at the hands of fighters when war finally broke out into full fury. The fact that medium bombers could not rely on speed alone to protect themselves from fighters also started many AAC and Boeing personnel thinking was their new aircraft truly a 'flying fortress'.

Boeing spent over $100,000 on getting the installation of the turbo-supercharger units correct on the Y1B-17A, and then to their surprise found that the AAC refused to pay the bill! Not overly pleased with having to 'bite the bullet' on such a large chunk of change, Boeing suggested to the AAC that they should put the turbo-supercharged model into production. The military duly took their advice, issuing a contract for ten new aircraft, with options for further bombers as part of the same deal.

The aircraft was initially given the designation Model 299E, but it incorporated so many changes that this was modified to Model 299M. Although looking externally similar to earlier Fortresses, the new B-17B boasted many changes including an entirely new nose section, which eliminated the kinked for-

This B-17B is a bit of a problem aircraft. Photographed on 16 July 1940 whilst being used as a test bed for the new Sperry gun turrets, the aircraft boasts some of the features of a B-17C (including flush waist gun position) which leads me to the conclusion that at least one B-model was updated to include features of the C-model. The shapes of the turrets can be seen directly behind the pilots' position and on the lower rear fuselage. Tufting has been applied to the rear fuselage and tail group to measure how the turrets would affect air flow

ward fuselage and deleted the rather useless rotating turret mounted in its extremity. The new section, while being more attractive in appearance, was seven inches shorter and saw the navigator/bombardier moved from his position behind the Y1B-17's pilots to a more practical forward position in the nose itself. New plexiglass panels were installed in the reconfigured nose section, with an optically-flat bomb aiming panel also built into the unit. Finally, a ball and socket mounting was fitted in the nose for the installation of a Browning .30-cal air-cooled machine gun.

Testing with the Y1B-17A had proven that more efficient exhausting could be created by mounting the ducting on the left and right sides of the inboard left and right engines respectively, and these changes became standard on the B-17B and subsequent aircraft. The wing's leading edge was also fitted with intake slots for supercharger induction, with intercooler air exiting through eight slots (on each wing panel) mounted behind the main wing spar.

The B-17B's brakes were hydraulic, and replaced the pneumatic system fitted to earlier variants. The longer flaps were now metal, rather than fabric, and covered, while the surface area of the ailerons was slightly decreased and that of the rudder slightly increased. The bomber was also made capable of carrying external bomb racks under the wing which could accommodate up to 2000 lbs of extra ordnance. A lengthening of the inboard wing section also saw an increase in area, but without an increase in total span.

The AAC was extremely anxious to get the new aircraft (plus the optional bombers) so that the high-altitude strategic bombing theories could be operationally tested and incorporated into a useful battle plan. Boeing accountants, in the meantime, had come to the startling revelation that the company was actually losing money on each aircraft built – so much for the dream of financial prosperity! When the new figures were presented, the AAC was more than unsympathetic, turning a deaf ear to Boeing proposals, and suggesting contracts could be cancelled if Boeing refused to honour the previously agreed prices.

Company officials duly travelled to Washington to argue with the AAC, who did not want to pay more than $198,000 per aircraft, while ignoring a previously agreed price of $205,000. Boeing claimed they would be losing money even at the higher rate! Tempers flared, and the new Chief of the AAC duly became embroiled in the dispute, Henry 'Hap' Arnold having been appointed to take the place of Gen Oscar Westover, who had been killed in an air crash. The former was more than sympathetic with the AAC desire to create a strategic bombing force, but other government officials were not so sure, and a real battle developed between the factions.

Finally, Boeing threatened to withdraw entirely from the B-17 programme, reasoning it could see little point in losing money on each order. However, company officials pared the price down as much as was possible, and an agreement was finally reached where by the AAC would pay $202,500 per aircraft. It was not the figure Boeing had desired, but at least it was

A ramp full of Fortress Is destined for the RAF. Aircraft were rolled out in natural metal finish with full RAF markings, although their rudders had already been daubed with camouflage paint

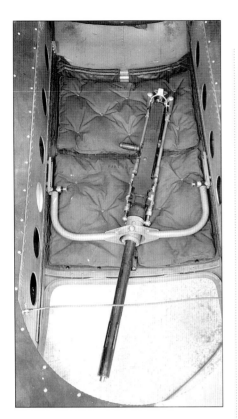

With the B-17C, armament was upgraded to the larger .50-cal Browning machine gun, although a smaller .30-cal weapon was still carried in the nose. The belly cupola was replaced with a larger 'bathtub', which gave a somewhat improved field-of-fire. This view is looking down into the bathtub, showing the quilted gunner's pad and simple mounting for the weapon

RIGHT The advent of the B-17D saw the bomber's armament increased yet again – an additional .50-cal was added to the upper and lower positions. This photograph, taken on 28 March 1941, shows the dual .50-cal Browning mount and ammunition trays. The field-of-fire was still rather restricted, however

a marginal improvement on $198,000. Company officials had, however, scored a big point in their favour by illustrating to the AAC the utter lack of cost-effectiveness in ordering small groups of bombers. Each side duly parted company a little happier than when they had first met, Boeing with more money and the AAC with a strategic bomber programme which was still intact.

However, back at the new Plant 2 building, which had been erected for B-17 and Stratoliner production, further economic problems were arising. Boeing was having serious trouble with the turbo-superchargers, for the GE units were failing at a very frequent rate, placing the whole high altitude programme once again in jeopardy. The turbos were extremely sensitive to heat and cold, and would crack if not correctly operated. There was also a disconcerting tendency for the units to burst into flames, starting a fire which could burn through the aluminium wing structure in just a matter of minutes.

The original contract for ten B-17Bs (quickly followed by the exercising of an option for an additional 29) was signed during November 1937, but the turbo-supercharger problems meant that the first aircraft did not fly until 27 June 1939. However, with these cured, deliveries proceeded fairly rapidly, with all 39 B-17Bs handed over to the AAC between 29 July 1939 and 30 March 1940 – a definite point in Boeing's favour.

This small force of 39 brand-new bombers gave the AAC enough aircraft to equip two bombardment groups – one on

either coast of the United States. The dependable 2nd BG swapped its Y1B-17s for B-17Bs at Langley Field, while the 7th BG 'set up shop' with its Boeing bombers at the picturesque Hamilton Field, located on San Francisco Bay.

Now that the AAC had its new strategic bombers, it only remained for them to develop an effective way of using the machines. However, they soon ran into all sorts of problems as the big bombers climbed towards their new operational ceilings, the intense cold at high altitude playing havoc on men and

The dual .50-cal installation in the B-17D's bathtub. This view is looking aft, and it can be clearly seen how armour plate has been mounted above and in front of the barrels. The addition of two guns to an already limited space restricted the gunner's field of view even more

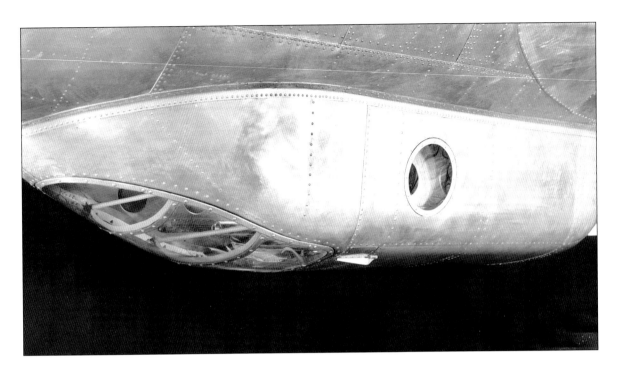

equipment, and rendering oil and other lubricants with the consistency of tar. Each problem had to be faced and then overcome, and many times these difficulties were solved simply by 'Yankee ingenuity', as crew chiefs came up with fixes and solutions which would have cost the government thousands of dollars if they had had to rely on private industry.

Once most of the problems were solved, the groups began to practice the new and arcane art of high-altitude bombing. At first the results were dismal, with crews not able to hit the proverbial barn, but slowly results improved as the bombardment groups, and their component squadrons, evolved into tight-knit fighting units. Throughout this period entirely new combat tactics were written in the skies over America as the units worked up to combat strength.

Boeing would later figure that they had lost $12,000 on *each* B-17B built, which was a major blow to a company that, although not exactly on the brink of financial disaster, was certainly worried about its economic future. However, even before the first B-17B had flown – and setting aside the various squabbles – the AAC knew that it needed to order more aircraft if the strategic bombing concept was to become an effective combat tool, rather than a technological showcase. Now powered by reliable turbo-supercharged engines, the B-17B was regularly attaining the altitudes the AAC required, and the development of a new bombsight also promised the accuracy that had, up to this point in the aircraft's career, been sorely missing.

The latter device, built by Norden, made use of gyroscopes and a bomb fall computing system which gave unparalleled accuracy. Oddly, this unit had initially been ordered by the

This exterior view shows the B-17C's bathtub position in close-up. When attacked, the gunner would clamber into the position on his stomach and then sight and fire the single .50-cal through the rear opening, very limited extra visibility being supplied by the small port holes in the sides of the position. Note the small wind deflector which automatically deployed when the weapon was extended. This photograph was taken on 16 September 1940

Navy, although the AAC quickly grabbed the bombsight as prize equipment for its fleet of Flying Fortresses once its accuracy was determined – from 10,000 ft, AAC bombardiers could regularly hit targets with the Norden device, although from 20,000 ft accuracy decreased accordingly. However, bombs could still be placed very near target areas even at the latter height, and the resulting destruction level was considered to be more than acceptable.

Turbo-supercharging and the Norden bombsight gave the AAC a sense that they had created a super bomber in the B-17B. The capability of flying at great heights also meant that most anti-aircraft fire could be avoided, while enemy fighters, if they had little warning, would be hard-pressed to reach the altitudes occupied by the B-17s before they had dropped their bombs. Unfortunately, technology levels, spurred on by the worsening political situation in Europe, were developing so rapidly that the concept of invulnerable bombing platforms quickly became obsolete once the 'shooting' war started.

The Germans, for example, had built the Messerschmitt Bf 109 fighter at around the same time as the B-17, and this machine had evolved through the addition of more powerful engines to the point where it could easily intercept high flying bombers from 'a standing start'. This performance, married with its formidable machine gun and cannon armament, made the Bf 109 more than a match for any unescorted bomber, including the B-17. However, Boeing and the AAC reasoned that if enough Flying Fortresses were massed into formations, then the covering fire provided by each machine's five .30-cal weapons could weave a protective umbrella of 'hot lead' through which fighter aircraft would have difficulty safely passing.

Once again this concept became questionable as the Germans and British developed highly accurate ground control stations which could vector swarms of fighters rapidly, and precisely, into the path of incoming bomber streams. Large formations also meant that the overall speed of the individual B-17s would have to be limited so that the integrity of defensive boxes could be maintained.

Although the press highlighted the 'flying fortress' concept, reality was rearing its ugly head in the changing face of aerial combat. Indeed, when visiting British and French aircraft purchasing delegations went to Seattle in 1940, they were not overly impressed with the Fortress's defensive armament. They found the gun cupolas cramped and the field-of-fire narrow, making it extremely difficult to track and fire at targets from these positions. Aircraft from both nations had suffered gravely at hands of the Luftwaffe's cannon-equipped fighters (a single cannon shell had proven capable of knocking down the largest aircraft with just one solid hit) during the May 1940 *Blitzkrieg*, which had seen the Germans 'steam-roller' their way across western Europe. Despite reservations over the bomber's defensive armament, and scepticism in respect to Boeing's combat

capability claims, the visiting delegations were nevertheless impressed with the 'Fort's' looks and performance.

Taking European recommendations to heart, the AAC attempted to make their next variant of the Boeing bomber more 'combat worthy'. The B-17C (Model 299H) immediately dispensed with the neat-looking cupolas on the sides of the fuselage in favour of streamlined plexiglass hatches which not only gave waist gunners a much better field of vision, but also more room to manoeuvre the weapon. Space for more ammunition was also provided for the waist guns, whilst the blister housing for the .30-cal belly weapon was deleted and, in its place, a 'bathtub' gunner's installation fitted, which once again greatly improved the field-of-fire and visibility.

At around this time reports emanating from Europe indicated that the .30-cal weapon was inadequate in many respects, although the British kept insisting on .303-cal guns, believing that a massed battery of these weapons would result in greater destructive power. The new B-17C duly had a single .50-cal fitted in the belly's 'bathtub' position, while a similar weapon was mounted in the radio compartment. Forward field of fire was still weak, however, with only one .30-cal on a ball and socket mounting being situated in the framed plexiglass nose.

The AAC ordered 38 B-17Cs, but this still did not give Boeing the mass-production capability it needed to order sup-

Assigned to the Air Material Division at Wright Field, this B-17C wears its controlling unit's 'MD' designation on the vertical tail and Wright Field's arrow on fuselage. This view also shows the black stripes indicating walkways atop the wing

plies in quantity, thus reducing overall price. The contract, which included the provision for spares, totalled in excess of $8 million, but this still did not help Boeing's financial problems for each aircraft was still built using a great deal of individual fitting work which detracted from the philosophy of mass production. The first C-model flew on 21 July 1940, but modifications were rapidly being added to the assembly line as combat reports from Europe were received and studied.

One of the most obvious points repeated again and again in the reports was the fact that aircraft not fitted with self-sealing fuel tanks were candidates for instant destruction. The punch of a heavy cannon or a burst of machine gun fire using incendiary ammunition was enough to turn the stoutest of aircraft into a bonfire when the machine was not equipped with self-sealing tanks – this type of tank was usually built out of rubber with some form of foam lining which was able to take a direct hit without sparking, and whose material was able to 'close up' around a bullet or cannon strike, preventing the spillage of fuel which could cause another fire risk. Wisely, self-sealing tanks were incorporated into the B-17C production line, and they would provide the bomber with a considerable margin of safety.

A further vital addition to the B-17C airframe was the use of armour plate for crew and systems protection. The concept of the Flying Fortress flying high and fast enough to evade flak and fighters was quickly forgotten with the advent of war. Boeing and the AAC were sobered by reports coming in from Europe which described instances of entire RAF bomber formations flying directly into the fury of the enemy with not one single aircraft returning! Realising that the B-17 would have to 'slug it out' with some of the best fighters ever built flown by seasoned pilots with plenty of combat experience, Boeing began adding chunks of armour plate to the C-model. At first, the use of armour was rather restrained, but this would shortly change.

Boeing had guessed correctly when figuring the Wright R-1820 would have lots of growth potential, and the B-17C was fitted with R-1820-65 radials which could develop a dependable 1200-hp each – the extra power pushed the C-model's top speed to 323 mph at 25,000 ft. The Wrights were excellent engines, offering low man-hour maintenance per flight hour, and were to prove dependable in the most foul of field condition.

When war broke out in Europe on 3 September 1939, the AAC had only 23 Flying Fortresses in its active inventory, and even before the first C-model had flown, the 'Corps was busy ordering another batch of Fortresses to bolster its very small force. Forty-two B-17Ds (Model 299H) were to be built, and these aircraft included certain modifications like the addition of cowl flaps to improve engine cooling, an improved electrical system and inclusion of yet another crew member, which raised the complement to ten. Otherwise, the B-17D looked nearly identical to the C-model.

The B-17D also boasted increased defensive armament, with the bathtub and radio compartment positions each receiving an additional .50-cal weapon. Both still enjoyed only limited visibility and field-of-fire, but the addition of these extra heavy weapons was a step in the right direction. Additional sockets were also provided in the nose compartment so that the .30-cal weapon could be relocated, or additional weapons added once in the frontline.

Bladder fuel tanks were installed, the internal bomb racks modified for improved operations and a low-pressure oxygen system fitted for the crew. The 12-volt electrical system was also replaced by a 24-volt system and myriad other smaller changes made to the aircraft as they were completed in Plant 2.

Delivery of D-models to the AAC started on 29 April 1941, with the last example being taken on charge on 10 September 1941. By this time, a major change had taken place for, in June 1941, the Air Corps had become the United States Army Air Force (USAAF).

By this stage the Roosevelt administration, realising the desperate position in which the British and French governments found themselves in 1939, agreed to sell aircraft to the nations on a 'cash and carry' basis. This was later revised into the famous Lend-Lease Bill (HR 1776). Both nations knew American-built aircraft were quite stout, but often lacked up-to-date performance, armour and armament, and were sometimes not blessed with the best handling characteristics. However, they were desperate for aircraft since their factories, working at maximum capacity, could not build the required aircraft for the war which everyone now realised was on its way.

After visiting the Seattle factory, Britain requested 20 B-17Cs for the RAF in late 1940. The Battle of Britain had come and gone, with the RAF prevailing in a bloody and costly campaign. Despite suffering heavy loses, the Luftwaffe was not about to give up on its assault on Britain however, and it changed tactics from day to night bombing, creating a new form of aerial warfare in the process. The night *blitz* on Britain had begun. For months on end, fleets of German aircraft roared over Britain striking a curious blend of targets. London was the sentimental favourite because of the propaganda value attached to striking at the British capital, this fixation the Nazi high command had with blasting vast acres of cities into blackened rubble saving numerous military targets like factories and airfields from sure destruction. By following such a course, the Luftwaffe not only allowed the RAF to make good its losses suffered during the Battle of Britain, but also stiffened the resolve of the general population against a possible German invasion.

An embryonic Bomber Command had also started to strike nack at German targets using Wellingtons, Whitleys and a variety of other medium and light bombers manned by courageous crews. They would venture out virtually every night and fly into the dangerous skies of 'Fortress Europe' in search of targets,

With its four Wrights at take-off power, a new B-17B climbs away from Boeing Field. The C-model would see the elimination of the streamlined, but not effective, side and belly gun cupolas

despite the fact that accurate night bombing was difficult at best, unless one had perfect guidance to target, or if the target was illuminated by flare or fires from previous bomb strikes – and there was always the threat of increasingly sophisticated German nightfighters and the very professional, and accurate, flak barrages. Having achieved poor results nocturnally for the reasons described, the RAF decided that they needed to try their hand at strategic bombing during daylight hours – hence the request for B-17Cs. However, at this time Boeing and the AAC told the British that the bomber was only suitable for training purposes until more combat-worthy aircraft became available.

Delivered to the RAF during the spring of 1941, the bombers were named Fortress Is (Boeing Model 299T) and finished in shiny overall natural aluminium. However, they were soon camouflaged in grey/green and assigned to No 90 Sqn at West Raynham, in Norfolk, following their transatlantic ferry flights. Period correspondence indicates that Boeing really thought that the aircraft were going to be utilised as four-engined trainers, but the RAF had other ideas.

The introduction of the Fortress I into European service went rather less than well – the first aircraft to arrive at West Raynham touched down too hard, went off the runway and tore off its landing gear. Despite this obvious incident of pilot error, No 90 Sqn's crews had actually been hand-picked for the job, with no individual being older than 24 and all aircrew having passed a decompression test to an altitude of 35,000 ft. Operating at such heights was to cause great hardship on the crews and the aircraft, and resulted in the bombers trailing long condensation plumes which made life easier for Luftwaffe fighters and flak crews alike.

Despite these problems, No 90 Sqn nevertheless had the honour of being the first unit to take the B-17 into combat, three Fortress Is being despatched for a trial raid to Wilhelmshaven on 8 July 1941. One of the bombers had to abort due to engine troubles, but the remaining two carried on, climbing to 30,000 ft and dropping their bombs over the target area. Equipped with Sperry bombsights rather than the more accurate Norden (which the American government would not release for foreign use), the Fortress Is' bombs failed to find their intended targets, and both aircraft were intercepted by fighters. Heading back to Britain at maximum speed, the crews were more than a little surprised to find their Brownings had frozen solid due to the dismally low temperatures at altitude.

After puzzling over their rather lack-lustre introduction to combat, No 90 Sqn launched its first official raid on 24 July against the port of Brest in order to sink the German battle-cruiser *Gneisenau*, which was moored in the harbour. Squadron aircraft once again came in at 30,000 ft dragging mile-long condensation trails, dropped their bombs and turned back for 'Blighty'. Fighters rose to do battle, and most of the Forts received some form of battle damage. One Fortress I actually broke apart when it landed back at base, the machine becoming a future 'parts depot' for other squadron aircraft (parts were in especially short supply from Boeing). The crews claimed strikes on targets, but this apparently was never verified.

Even though operations were difficult, and results generally disappointing, the RAF quickly realised that the Fortress I could absorb a great deal of battle damage and return to base.

A raid was set up to attack targets in the Norwegian port of Narvik, but before this could be stage a Fortresses was burned to the ground by a fire which had started while the bomber was undergoing maintenance. Three Fortress Is nevertheless headed out at high altitude to hit Narvik – but none came back. All three were apparently intercepted and shot down.

Back in Britain, disaster continued to plague No 90 Sqn. One Fortress crashed after coming apart at altitude during a test flight, whilst another dove out of a low cloud base near the airfield and hit the ground, killing the crew. Missions continued on a limited scale (22 were eventually flown), but trouble continued to follow the bomber and the RAF decided to stop daylight raids during September. The unit got rid of its Fortress Is and received Short Stirlings for the night mission instead.

The surviving Fortress Is were scattered, four going to the Middle East, where they attacked targets at night. By October 1941, the few Fortress Is still in Britain were transferred to Nos 206 and 220 Sqns of Coastal Command, where they operated in a recon and anti-submarine role. During its operational period, the Fortress I was found to have inadequate defensive fire power, insufficient armour and the inability to cope with the extremely low temperatures found at 30,000 ft. On the plus side, pilots found the big Boeing a very pleasant aircraft to fly, and the cockpit seemed to be very well designed for combat operations. Other sources in Britain suggested that the bomber was incapable of operations over Europe, while several observers went as far as to suggest the Americans should build bombers of British design and drop the Fortress completely. The combat debut of the B-17 had been less than successful.

Back at home, Boeing and the military were more than alarmed by the disastrous results of these high-altitude missions. All B-17Cs remaining in the inventory were brought up to rough B-17D standard with extra guns, revised electrical systems and more armour.

Realising the situation was equally critical in the Philippines, the USAAF despatched most of the B-17D force to the 19th BG. Arriving in the island nation after an epic ferry flight, the bombers were stationed at Del Monte and Clark Fields while the crews began training and familiarisation flights around the area.

The bombers' beautiful polished natural metal finish (maintained in impeccable condition by the pre-war AAC) gave given way to Olive Drab and Neutral Grey camouflage in an attempt to offer some form of protective colouration. The 19th BG had a total of 33 Flying Fortresses on the ground on 8 December 1941 when Japan attacked the main bases on the islands with a resounding fury. Eighteen of the bombers were destroyed on the ground in the stunning attack that caught the Americans by surprise. Many other aircraft were damaged, but heroic groundcrews managed to patch up most of them, and the 19th BG began a rearguard action, attacking the enemy whenever possible and causing considerable damage while delaying Japanese plans for the occupation of the Philippines.

In Hawaii, B-17s were caught on the ground and destroyed during the attack of 7 December (the date difference between the Philippines and Hawaiian attacks was due to the International Date Line). Twelve brand-new B-17E Flying Fortresses were actually on the last leg of a ferry flight from California to Hawaii when the attack took place, and they found themselves in the unfortunate position of arriving over the islands whilst both sides were still blazing away at each other. Because of the need to carry extra fuel and supplies, the 12 bombers lacked armament, making then sitting ducks for the marauding Japanese Zeros. However, not one was downed, although several were badly damaged and had to force-land.

Thus, America was left with just a handful of B-17s in Hawaii that would take some work to bring up to combat status, and a small force in the Philippines which was doing its best to maul the enemy while avoiding being blasted into oblivion by a numerically superior foe. The bomber's initiation into combat with the USAAF had been little less than a major disaster.

CHAPTER 3 BIG TAIL BIRD

BOEING'S FURTHER TESTING with the B-17C/D, along with the RAF's less than successful experience with the Fortress I, led both the manufacturer and the AAF to drastically revise their specification for the bomber. While undoubtedly elegant and streamlined in the best Art Deco fashion, the early Forts lacked so much in the way of combat-worthiness that a complete redesign of the fuselage, and a rethinking of the strategic bomber's role, was necessary.

Combat over Europe had proven that the B-17 could not escape enemy flak or outgun enemy interceptors. The Fortress I's record of 39 bombing missions with only two recorded hits and eight aircraft lost in operations was not acceptable, and resulted in a disagreement arising between the RAF and the Americans. The latter blamed the British for not flying correct defensive formations, whilst the RAF countered with the statement that the bomber was not suited to European operations.

The AAF advocated that a tight bombing formation was necessary to allow the bombers' guns to support each aircraft in the formation. The British tended to string their aircraft along in a non-formation basis, each bomber commander being individually responsible for attacking and hitting the target. As is usual with these types of arguments, both sides had their positive points. The RAF *was* ignoring the bombing techniques for which the aircraft had been designed, while the Fortress I *did* have inadequate armament and combat equipment.

In order for the Flying Fortress to be an effective strategic bomber, its defensive firepower had to be increased dramatically, while lots of internal combat equipment was also needed. The answer to these vexing problems would be the B-17E (Model 299-O, a designation which was, oddly, also applied to the later F- and G-models). On 17 June 1940, an order for 150 of the new models was signed, finally giving Boeing the numbers they needed for mass-production, along with a possible profit. There was a dark side to this contract, however, for earlier in the year Boeing had made a commitment for stocks of materials from suppliers, since they figured a new order would be forthcoming. But the military did not react as quickly as

Boeing thought they would, and the company had to cancel contracts with suppliers, thus losing money.

A bright point occurred on 12 July when the military upped its order to 277 aircraft, whilst a 16 September amendment added a further 235 B-17Es. Despite going from famine to feast, Boeing *still* had its accounting problems, and the company and AAF haggled as to the exact price of the bomber, and it was not until 8 August that the Secretary of War gave his approval to the *first* order. By the time the dust settled, the B-17E would cost the military approximately $300,000 each – and Boeing was still worried that they would be losing money.

The company had to place huge orders for supplies, but when they did, they found that even larger orders had also been placed by other aviation concerns, as they too tooled up to fill war orders. Aluminium, in particular, was in huge demand, and the government had to quickly organise a war emergency plan to supply the defence industry with needed material.

Since design work during that time period moved at a very rapid pace, a wooden mock-up of a new fuselage was constructed in a Boeing hangar. Aft of the wing, the new fuselage was completely different from previous Forts, and it had to be in order to incorporate all the improvements required by the military. To create the B-17E, over 400 changes had to be made to the basic design concept by chief B-17 designer Edward C Wells and his team.

With the B-17E, Boeing was finally able to put into place mass-production techniques for their four-engined bomber – the lack of which had caused the company to loose money on the earlier Flying Fortresses built. Boeing also began dramatically increasing the size of its work force, and this meant hiring many women, since more and more men were joining up in the prelude to war. This view shows five such employees on their Cushman motor scooters, which were utilised to deliver small parts, mail and inter-company orders and memoranda. In the background, mechanics prepare a B-17E for its acceptance flights. Note the offset ADF (Air Direction Finding) 'football', as well as the twin pitot tubes and ball and socket mountings for the nose area machine guns

An experimental and test department had been established by Boeing with the influence of Edmund T 'Eddie' Allen, who had joined the company in 1937. When a company like Boeing had reached the testing stage for a new aircraft, it was then standard practice to hire a freelance test pilot, or obtain help from the AAC. While there was nothing wrong with this practice, it not develop a solid technical/testing base within the company. Since Allen was a test pilot, he felt strongly that these functions needed to come in-house, and he was subsequently appointed Director of Aerodynamics and Flight Research, helping to establish the use of wind tunnels for test work at Boeing.

Allen had tested the Boeing 307 pressurised four-engined airliner and felt that the aircraft lacked directional stability. The aircraft had a vertical tail not unlike that on the early Forts, but Allen had the unit redesigned into a much more substantial structure, thus curing the stability problems. A similar tail was eventually adopted for the B-17E, along with a larger horizontal stabiliser, which had an elevator ten feet longer than the unit on the B-17D.

The wooden mock-up fuselage was six feet longer than previous models, since a gunner's position had to be fitted into the extreme tail position. The adoption of the latter was the direct result of lessons learned in combat, the virtually naked tail of the bomber needing protection from attacks by fighters. The gun position (not really a turret since it was not powered) was its own sub-assembly, with seating for the gunner, his two machine guns, ammunition and sighting equipment. Armament was also increased as a powered turret was added directly behind the flightdeck, thus effectively eliminating what had once been a fairly roomy position. The turret chosen for fitment was the Sperry A-1 unit – a substantial piece of equipment fitted with two .50-cal machine guns. Although only a small

What a collector's item this would make! Beautifully handmade from laminated woods, this wind tunnel model was created to test the reshaped B-17E, and was photographed on 4 December 1940. The model was used to verify the aerodynamics of the new rear fuselage, as well as the top and belly turrets

plexiglass dome protruded from the top of the fuselage, the turret mechanism stood 7 ft 6 in high, had a diameter of 41 in and weighed in at nearly 700 lbs. It was a formidable piece of equipment that would greatly add to the Fort's defensive profile, and was fed by six magazines, each holding 125 rounds.

As previously mentioned, the bathtub belly gun position on early Forts was quite inadequate, and with the B-17E, Boeing attempted to rectify the situation. Bendix supplied a low profile solid turret for the belly, fitted with two .50-cal guns. This was a remotely-controlled device run by a gunner who lay on his stomach facing aft while sighting the turret through a series of angled mirrors fitted to a periscope device housed in a clear bubble a few feet aft of the turret itself! This arrangement was as complex to use as it is to describe.

The side gunners' positions were retained, but in a much-modified form. The newly-widened fuselage gave the gunners more room, and each side had a post-mounted .50-cal weapon directly opposite the other. Initially, each weapon was fed by two large metal containers that held 100 rounds each, but these were eventually discarded in favour of a simplified belt-fed system. Each fuselage position had a large plexiglass window that could slide forward when the gunners were ready for action. Also, a small wind deflector made movement of the weapon in the slipstream easier, although it did nothing to reduce the freezing temperatures to which the gunners were subjected.

The B-17E admittedly lost the grace of the earlier Forts, but it traded in its good looks for a utilitarian aggressiveness which

Fine inflight study of the very first B-17E (41-2393), which was flown in bare metal finish. Powered by Wright R-1820-65s, the E-model was ordered on 30 August 1940 and this aircraft flew on 5 September 1941. Note that the turret and rudder have been painted in Olive Drab – this aircraft was latter camouflaged overall. It was written off in a crash in Newfoundland in early January 1942

LEFT A pre-made wooden seat offers a touch more comfort for this Boeing employee working inside a B-17E engine nacelle which is mounted vertically on a jig. Once her task had been completed, she would move on to the next wing, taking her seat and tool box with her

BELOW These gleaming objects are B-17E fuel tanks which are receiving some final finishing work. The 'bullet proof' fuel cell, which was made out of a rubberised material, was fitted inside these metal tanks once construction of the latter was completed

BELOW A Boeing inspector checks out a supply of B-17E outer wing panels before they head for mating with an aircraft. Photographed during 1942, this view perfectly illustrates how Boeing was finally able to achieve mass-production with the Flying Fortress. Also of note is that the bare metal panels have been sprayed with the national insignia in advance of being camouflaged. Once mated, the entire aircraft would be sprayed in Olive Drab and Neutral Grey

would stand the AAF much better in combat. The addition of a tail gun as well as power turrets (America had become the world leader in turret technology – the RAF and Luftwaffe lagged far behind) greatly increased the bomber's defensive posture. The large diameter fuselage would also, of course, increase the aircraft's drag coefficient (as well as weight) but, through careful designing, Boeing managed to make the expanded fuselage as 'tight' as possible so a tail gunner (preferably of small stature!) could be carried, while retaining the majority of the bomber's performance figures.

The broader fuselage, larger tail and additional turrets only imposed a six mph speed penalty upon the E-model – an out-

ABOVE B-17E construction number 113 (41-2505) displays its new Sperry belly turret – a piece of equipment that would make the Fortress a more formidable weapon. This photograph was taken on 5 February 1942, some three weeks after its delivery by Boeing to the AAF's Portland depot. Five days later it was assigned to the 19th BG and sent to Java, only to be posted missing in action (MIA), along with its eight crewmen, over New Guinea on 25 April 1942

LEFT The addition of the electrically-operated top turret to the B-17E greatly increased the aircraft's defensive capabilities. The gunner had a much-improved field-of-fire (this would get better in later models, as much of the turret bracing was eliminated), allowing the twin .50-cal Brownings to be brought to bear on attacking targets with greater effectiveness

standing achievement considering the large improvement in the bomber's capabilities. In order to compensate for the added drag of the turrets, the E-model had a retractable tail wheel, which slightly reduced overall drag. Equipped with a minimum of eight .50-cal and at least two .30-cal guns (nose and radio compartment), the B-17E was now a potent weapon. The nose armament had remained the same, the AAF figuring, incorrectly, that an enemy fighter would never try a head-on attack with such fast closing speeds between the two aeroplanes.

Because of problems hiring new personnel, erecting new facilities at Boeing Field and an erratic supply of materials, Boeing started to fall behind on the delivery of the B-17E. The first aircraft took to the air on 27 September 1941 instead of the contract date of 30 April. However, through a maximum effort, the company would make up the lost time as the B-17E production rate increased, and the final aircraft in the contract would actually be delivered well ahead of schedule. Even with this much larger production run of aircraft, there was still a great deal of individual hand-fitting on the line but nothing like the amount of man hours that had to be expended on the earlier machines. Boeing was well on its way to achieving the hoped-for mass-production, but the increasing pressure of war would introduce a unique new concept for building bombers.

The demand for Flying Fortresses was now so great that Boeing realised it could not fulfil the ever-increasing orders. Accordingly, a new plan was created to bring other manufacturers into the B-17 production stream, namely the Vega Division of Lockheed Aircraft at Burbank Airport and Douglas

Flying near a snow-capped and cloud shrouded Mt Rainier, B-17E 41-2599 makes for an imposing study during a pre-delivery check flight from the Boeing plant. Delivered to the AAF's Lowry depot on 26 February 1942, this aircraft was initially assigned to the 93rd BS/19th BG in Hawaii, before being transferred to the 65th BS/43rd BG. Whilst with the latter unit it was dubbed *Tugboat Annie* and participated in the Battle of Midway, before being lost when it ditched in the Pacific on 16 January 1943

Aircraft at Long Beach. In April 1941, Courtland and Robert Gross of Lockheed entered into discussions with Maj-Gen Oliver P Echols about the possibility of producing the Flying Fortress under license. Realising their proposed new civilian airliners would probably be drastically affected by the coming of the war, the pair saw the obvious merit in joint production of the bombers.

Lockheed received a B-17E pattern aircraft, blueprints and a certain amount of tooling and loaned technical expertise from Boeing. Increasing its work force for the various plants surrounding the Lockheed Air Terminal, the company went to work with a vengeance on preparing to produce new bombers. Further south, Douglas was doing the same at Long Beach.

Around 100 B-17Es had been delivered to the AAF by 7 December 1941, but not all of these machines had been brought up to the latest combat standards. During the attack, six B-17Es of the 88th Reconnaissance Squadron (RS) and six B-17Cs of the 38th RS flew right into the war while on a ferry flight from Hamilton Field to Hawaii. Unfortunately, none of the aircraft were armed, and the majority received some form of damage, while several had forced landings. The Forts which were not destroyed on the ground the Philippines and in Hawaii were almost immediately sent on combat patrols. The Japanese felt that bombers would be excellent targets since they were so large, not realising just how structurally tough the Boeing product was, nor fully appreciating, at first, just how clever Americans were at sticking machine guns into every 'nook and cranny' on the Forts. The enemy also did not realise that most Forts were equipped with self-sealing fuel tanks and armour pro-

The prototype B-17E is seen outside its hangar on a foggy night in Seattle. With America's entry into World War 2, the rather wonderful neon sign that adorned Boeing's B-17 assembly plant would pass into history. As can be seen, swing-shift work continues on other B-17Es inside the hangar – indicative that Boeing had finally achieved the mass-production the company had so long desired

tection – something the Japanese would not have themselves until the situation had reversed, and the addition of new combat equipment proved futile at best.

Japanese fighter pilots (some of the most highly trained and combat experienced in the world at that time) were amazed when attack after attack on Fortresses over the Philippines seemed to produce little result. Actually, the bombers were being repeatedly hit by the enemy's standard fighter fit of two rifle calibre machine guns (the cannon on the Zero was another matter, however), but the size of the bullet was such that if vital areas of the Fort were not destroyed, nor heavily damaged, the aircraft could carry on with their mission and return to base for rapid repairs. It was common for B-17s returning from missions against the Japanese to make a strange whistling sound, caused by the airflow rushing through the many bullet holes puncturing the aluminium skin.

With the start of America's actual involvement in World War 2, the flow of B-17Es to overseas bases began in earnest. Eight Forts headed toward the Canal Zone in December, whilst he B-17Es of the 7th BG departed Salt Lake City on the 5th of

Three female workers tackle the labour-intensive task of fitting out the interior of a very bare B-17E fuselage

the month for the Philippines. The events of 48 hours later quickly changed the situation, and six of the group's Forts were rushed to Hawaii, while the remaining 29 took up station in California in order to fend off a possible Japanese invasion.

Earlier model Forts headed to Spokane with the 39th BG in order to help defend the Northwest, whilst a paltry two B-17Bs flew further north to Alaska to provide the absolute minimum strategic capability for the 'roof of the world'. Apparently, military planners felt Alaska was safe from attack – they would soon find they were very, very wrong.

Fourteen tired and battered B-17s from the 19th BG fought all the way from the Philippines to Australia in a retreat which covered thousands of miles. They found that confusion reigned supreme in the latter country as the enemy made strategic raids on towns in the north-west of the vast island nation. The combat veteran Forts were quickly repaired, while their worn-out crews told horror stories to the men in newly-arriving E-models of the 7th BG. The latter group, comprising B-17Es and obsolete Consolidated LB-30s, combined with some of the left-over Philippine veterans and headed for Java for more bloody fighting with the Japanese. After losing the fight in Java, the survivors of the group flew on to India to re-equip and carry on the battle.

With its long-range capabilities, the B-17 carefully shadowed the enemy, reporting back vital intelligence on ship and troop movement. Since there were so few aircraft available, strike 'forces' of three to four aircraft were common, and the bombing results were not overly impressive.

As mentioned, the enemy had developed considerable respect for the tail gun position in the B-17E, resulting in new tactics being devised that saw enemy pilots making 'impossible' head-on attack, exposing the bomber to damaging gun fire in its least protected or defended area. This situation was soon remedied by the addition of as many forward firing guns as crews chiefs could cram into the nose. The early remote belly turret proved to be unreliable in frontline service, and quite often it was disassembled and removed, being replaced by a swivel mount with two machine guns firing through the open space left by the removal of the turret.

From the 113th production B-17E onwards, the troublesome Bendix belly turret system was replaced with the new Sperry ball turret. Electrically-operated, the turret had the gunner wrapped inside with a reflector gun sight between his feet. The turret could be moved very quickly, and proved to be an operational success, exacting a heavy toll on the enemy, and adding a new weapon to the inventory of the Fortress.

The Sperry turret did have its drawbacks, however. Since the entry door was at the gunner's back, he had to be placed in the turret by another crew member when the bomber was in flight. If the Fort was hit, the door would have to be released, allowing the gunner to crawl back into the fuselage. Belly turret

BLK. 10

ABOVE One of the main combat additions to the B-17E was the complete redesign of the rear fuselage to include a tail gunner's position and twin .50-cal Brownings. This factory view, taken on 1 October 1941, shows the ring and bead sight as well as the bolt-on external armour plate

RIGHT The rather cramped quarters for the B-17E tail gunner

gunners had to be very small people since there was so little room available – space did not permit wearing a parachute and, once out of the turret, the gunner would have to strap on his 'chute and attempt to escape the stricken bomber. Needless to say, casualties among the belly turret gunners were high.

Even though there was a tremendous urgency to get the B-17E into production, it is interesting to note that only approximately 160 examples saw combat. The majority went from the production line to training units to accommodate the massive need for crewmen. Of those sent to the frontline, most ended up in the Pacific, where they offered a token resistance to a successful and aggressive enemy, and few survived the rigours of combat.

The B-17E would, however, make history in Britain. On 1 July 1942, the first Forts of the 97th BG touched down in

Britain, having lost four of its forty-nine aircraft during the epic Atlantic crossing. The 97th was assigned to Polebrook, in Northamptonshire, once home to the Fortress Is of the RAF's No 90 Sqn.

Brig-Gen Ira C Eaker was the commander of VIII Bomber Command, and he wanted to get the Forts into action as soon as possible. However, the crews needed training, and the Americans subsequently had a hard time acclimatising to British and European weather conditions – far different from the normal blue skies associated with the stateside training bases. Norden bombsights were very difficult to use in the cloudy and hazy conditions often encountered, and the bombardiers discovered they needed some degree of ground visibility to successfully utilise this equipment. Also, it became obvious that the aircraft's rather limited bomb load (especially when compared to some of the British bombers) might prove to be a real liability in long-range missions.

On 17 August, training gave way to the first operational mission when Col Frank Armstrong, commanding officer of the 97th, took twelve E-models on a mission to Rouen-Sotteville – the importance of the raid was such that even Brig-Gen Eaker went along in another B-17. Seven more missions followed in short order, and as the bombers only encountered light anti-aircraft and fighter opposition, the flights were considered quite successful. Even though future missions would be extremely tough, and the whole concept of daylight strategic bombing would be reconsidered, the B-17 groups had taken their first real swing at 'Fortress Europe' and, from that point on, they would never be turned back.

B-17E 41-2656 received the name "Chief Seattle" at the factory. Naming ceremonies were quite common during the war since they provided good press coverage and served as a morale booster for the general public as well as the workers. "Chief Seattle" was assigned to the 19th BG's 435th BS on 29 May 1942 and was posted MIA during a reconnaissance mission over the Pacific on 19 August 1942

Superhuman escort
to victory...and beyond

"THE INVISIBLE CREW"

Beside our fighting men, in planes and ships and tanks, there rides an escort...invisible, superhuman ...magnifying their senses of sight and hearing... multiplying the strength of their avenging arms. It is "THE INVISIBLE CREW" of Bendix.

Equipped with "THE INVISIBLE CREW" ... all our Vehicles of Victory become the Transports of Tomorrow. Those tanks have Bendix Radio* equipment and Pioneer* instruments that make them land-navigating brothers of the Bendix-equipped ships at sea. Jeeps and trucks have their "INVISIBLE CREW,"

including revolutionary brake systems about which you will hear much. And in a big bomber, more than 200 Invisible Crewmen serve through every flight ... from the first impulse of Eclipse* starters, to easy stops on Bendix* Pneudraulic Landing Gear.

These creations of Bendix engineering, now mass-produced by many thousand precision workers in more than 30 plants, are helping to carry the war to the enemy on all fronts. And "THE INVISIBLE CREW" will serve a whole New Age of Transportation. This SUPERHUMAN ESCORT rides to Victory, and beyond.

SOME FAMOUS MEMBERS OF "THE INVISIBLE CREW"
PIONEER* Flight Instruments. BENDIX RADIO* Avigation, Detection, Communication Equipment. STROMBERG* Aircraft Injection Carburetors. ECLIPSE* AVIATION Starters, Auxiliaries. ECLIPSE MACHINE Starter Drives. SCINTILLA* Aircraft Ignition. BENDIX* PRODUCTS Stromberg Automotive Carburetors, Landing Gear. FRIEZ* Weather Instruments. ZENITH* Carburetors. BENDIX MARINE* Controls.

THE INVISIBLE CREW
PRECISION
EQUIPMENT BY
Bendix
Aviation Corporation

*TRADE MARKS OF BENDIX AVIATION CORPORATION OR SUBSIDIARIES COPYRIGHT 1943, BENDIX AVIATION CORPORATION

THE VEHICLES OF VICTORY...ARE THE TRANSPORTS OF TOMORROW

Bendix, "THE INVISIBLE CREW", May 1943

ONE ROUND TRIP
TO BERLIN ...
1100 GALLONS !

On a round trip from London to Berlin a Fortress may use about 1100 gallons of gasoline. A thousand heavy bombers need a million gallons of aviation gasoline to raid Frankfurt.

You see, to the airmen of this war, distance is measured more truly in gallons than in miles!

When our petroleum industry volunteered to produce *enough* gallons for total air war, we took on a whale of a big job. This is to report that we're seeing it through.

The Texas Company alone has delivered millions, *yes — hundreds of millions* of gallons of 100-octane aviation gasoline.

Texaco scientists developed a "liquid-catalyst isomerization" process. This process converts plentiful butane into precious isobutane, a vital material used in the production of aviation gasoline.

You'll benefit from Texaco's wartime research. And you won't have to wait for some future super-engine. Just wait 'til your Texaco Dealer gets his finer, more powerful post-war FIRE-CHIEF and SKY CHIEF gasolines!

THE TEXAS COMPANY

Coming ... finer **FIRE-CHIEF** *and* Sky Chief
gasolines because of Texaco's research in this war

Texaco, *ONE ROUND TRIP TO BERLIN ... 1100 GALLONS!*, June 1943

New Zone of Destruction
A new Super Fuel will create!

Censorship prohibits use of actual distance figures—but the zone map above tells part of the biggest gasoline story of the war!...

Just as fast as American refineries can get into production of a sensational new aviation gasoline—United Nations' bomber fleets will be given a new—far wider cruising range for their deadly blows at Axis Europe!

So powerful it can't be measured by the present 100 Octane yardstick—this new super fuel was born in a Socony-Vacuum laboratory—the result of two great petroleum advances—Socony-Vacuum's new TCC Process—and a sensational new Bead Catalyst!

Its extra power, which we call *Flying Horsepower*—will not only permit wider bombing range—but will give a new, quick maneuverability, speed, climbing power and carrying capacity to all types of United Nations' war planes.

The new processes which will make this super power possible, have been made available to the United States Government and to the entire petroleum industry—and 7 new Socony-Vacuum refining units are being installed.

Providing *Flying Horsepower* to help speed Victory—is just another Friendly Service to America from the Sign of the Flying Red Horse.

SOCONY-VACUUM OIL CO., INC., and Affiliates: Magnolia Petroleum Co., General Petroleum Corp. of California.

Mobilgas

SOCONY-VACUUM

TUNE IN RAYMOND GRAM SWING—Blue Network Coast-to-Coast, 10 P.M., E.W.T., Mon. Tues. Wed. Thurs.

Coming—
In Mobilgas *Flying Horsepower!* New Super Power for U.S. Planes

Mobilgas, *New Zone of Destruction*, July 1943

Have 2 Extra on Us, Tojo!

Thanks to *Flying Horsepower*— U. S. Bombers will be able to carry far heavier loads!

It's the greatest gasoline story of the war!...

How Socony-Vacuum scientists, working in a laboratory, found a way to produce a new super fuel *that will help the United Nations' great bomber fleets carry hundreds of extra tons of bombs to blast the way to Victory!*

The secret is a "magic" bead—Socony-Vacuum's new Bead Catalyst. It is so far superior to any catalyst heretofore used in gasoline refining—that even when diluted the fuel stock yields far greater power and performance than present 100 Octane gasoline.

This sensational discovery, coupled with Socony-Vacuum's new TCC Process, which permits *continuous* catalytic cracking—will not only *improve the quality,* but also *increase the quantity* of America's vital 100 Octane aviation gasoline!

This remarkable fuel of the future will give to aircraft a new,

quick maneuverability, speed, and carrying capacity...and already the new processes which make it possible have been made available to the U. S. Government and to the entire petroleum industry.

Thus, the United Nations' air fleets will be given a new power for Victory—*Flying Horsepower,* from the Sign of the Flying Red Horse!

SOCONY-VACUUM OIL CO., INC., and Affiliates: Magnolia Petroleum Co., General Petroleum Corp. of California

Mobilgas
SOCONY-VACUUM

TUNE IN RAYMOND GRAM SWING—Blue Network Coast-to-Coast, 10 P.M., E.W.T., Mon. Tues. Wed. Thurs.

Coming— In Mobilgas *Flying Horsepower!* New Super Power for U. S. Planes

Mobilgas, *Have 2 Extra on Us, Tojo!*, August 1943

≈ Reprinted by request ≈

Many requests have been received for copies of this dramatic Flying Fortress picture. Reprints, 24 x 22 inches, free from advertising, are now available on a special heavy stock suitable for framing. If you wish one, address Studebaker, South Bend, Indiana, enclosing 10¢ to cover mailing cost.

When the above Flying Fortress picture was first published in Studebaker advertisements last Fall, America's air might was just beginning to be felt in the Pacific and European war theaters. Today the Flying Fortress is spearheading one successful offensive operation after another. And every Studebaker man, who is privileged to help build Wright Cyclone engines for this invincible dreadnaught of the skies, follows the news of Flying Fortress victories with justifiable personal gratification in a job well done. Besides producing large quantities of Wright Cyclone engines for this devastating Boeing bomber, Studebaker is also turning out much other war matériel, including tens of thousands of big, multiple-drive military trucks.

Studebaker feels highly honored by the extent and the consequence of its assignments in the arming of our Nation and its Allies.

BUY U.S. WAR BONDS

Studebaker BUILDS WRIGHT CYCLONE ENGINES FOR THE *Flying Fortress*

Studebaker, *Reprinted by request*, September 1943

THROWING OUT THE "CABBAGE" AT 85° BELOW...

...can help speed sub-zero starting in your post-war car

Bombing our enemies from seven miles up involves many problems you'd never dream of...

It's cold...sometimes it hits 85° below zero. Gear lubricants often stick...bomb-bay doors refuse to open...controls don't work. A perilous trip may be wasted.

The Petroleum Industry was called upon to remedy this desperate problem...Texaco went to work immediately and in record time developed a brand new lubricant that won't "freeze" even in the paralyzing cold of the sub-stratosphere.

A technical victory...one of the many in Texaco's intensive war program. And these achievements...in making new war lubricants...vast amounts of 100-octane aviation gasoline...will help us give you even finer Texaco gasolines and lubricants to use in your post-war car.

You're welcome at
TEXACO DEALERS

Texaco, *THROWING OUT THE "CABBAGE" AT 85° BELOW*, October 1943

© 1944, The Studebaker Corporation

"Those engines sure have the power!"

THE brother of a waist gunner on a Boeing Flying Fortress wrote Studebaker quoting him as saying:

"Those Wright Cyclone engines that Studebaker builds are really dependable and sure have the power."

Comments like that are fully appreciated, of course. But Studebaker men and women know that what count most are the accomplishments of the stout-hearted air crews and rugged ground crews of our country's warplanes and the achievements of our fighting forces everywhere.

In fact, whatever amount of satisfaction the Studebaker organization may derive from the extent and consequence of its war work is always tempered by the realization that Studebaker is only one unit in a vast American fighting and producing team where everyone's effort is important.

Studebaker takes pride in its assignments on that team. Huge quantities of Wright Cyclone engines for the Boeing Flying Fortress—big multiple-drive military trucks—and other units of vital war matériel continue to stream forth from the five great Studebaker factories.

Unsung Hero

OF OUR NAVY

Aerial radio gunner in a Navy dive bomber! One of the toughest jobs of all! Let's show him we're for him and

BUY MORE BONDS

Studebaker BUILDS WRIGHT CYCLONE ENGINES FOR THE BOEING FLYING FORTRESS

Studebaker, *"Those engines sure have the power!"*, June 1944

Guardian Angels

The fireworks are all over. The "Sad Sack" is nearly home. A few minutes more, and she'll put her crew down safe on a friendly field.

She went out this morning full of fight, with her belly full of bombs . . . all four motors roaring defiance at every German in Italy.

She hammered the Nazi railyards at Terni, and left them a tangle of wreckage.

But she had to take a few on the chin to do it.

1ST LT. DONALD J. JUSTER, of St. Albans, N. Y. . . . Air Medal with 9 Oak Leaf Clusters. Bombardier of the Flying Fortress the "Sad Sack" . . .

"I'll say an escort of fighter planes is a mighty sweet sight to see! It's like the old Wild West movies— when the wagon train is surrounded by Indians and the cavalry rides to the rescue! Bombers and fighters, working together, make the A.A.F. an unbeatable team. And if you don't think so, take a look at Germany's big industrial centers from the air."

1ST LT. JOHN D. JOYCE, of Griffith, Indiana . . . Air Medal with 10 Clusters, Distinguished Flying Cross recommended . . . P-38 Pilot.

"I've helped escort the 'Sad Sack' on many a bombing mission . . . and seen Don Juster bullseye his bombs on plenty of Jerry objectives. And I want to tell you that's when teamwork pays off . . . teamwork between fighter pilots, between fighters and bombers, between members of bomber crews . . . teamwork that makes the A.A.F. the 'greatest team in the world'!"

When the escort fighters picked her up, the "Sad Sack" was on the spot . . . straggling behind her formation, with one engine knocked out by flak . . . trying to fight off a Focke-Wulf pack that was swarming in for the kill.

The sweetest sight her crew ever saw was that escort of P-38's . . . screaming down to the rescue with their noseguns squirting fire . . . chasing the Jerries out of there or shooting them down in flames.

That's why bomber-men call them "Guardian Angels", these escort fighter planes. For they bring back bombers and bomber crews to fly and fight again!

And that's the kind of team *you'll* be on when you wear A.A.F. wings . . . Pilots, Navigators, Bombardiers, Gunners, doing their job *together* . . . flying and fighting for the *team*, "the greatest team in the world!"

U. S. ARMY RECRUITING SERVICE

FLY AND FIGHT WITH THE **GREATEST TEAM IN THE WORLD**

AAF
ARMY AIR FORCES

AAF, *Guardian Angels*, November 1944

CHAPTER 4 SKY ROAD TO BERLIN

THE ARMY AIR FORCE originally ordered 812 B-17E bombers from Boeing, but following the completion of 512 E-models, the remainder of the contract was transferred to the production of the B-17F – an aircraft considered to be the first truly combat-ready Fort. This point can be debated since the B-17E really did participate most effectively in some very heavy fighting during the early part of the war.

The main identifying point of the B-17F over the E-model was the clear plexiglass nose dome which greatly improved visibility (however, some B-17Es were retrofitted with the dome, which confuses identification). Even though they looked alike, internal changes ran into the thousands, making the F-model a superior aircraft. The first 300 B-17Fs were purchased by contract AC-16, whilst contract W535-AC-20292 called for a further 3735, of which 1435 were completed as B-17Gs. Vega received contract AC-20290, while the Douglas contract was AC-20291.

The B-17F was fitted with new Wright R-1820-97 Cyclones that could pump out 1380 horsepower at war emergency settings, transferring the power through new paddle blade propellers made by Hamilton Standard – the props had a diameter of 11 ft 7 in. The cowlings were also slightly modified to accommodate changes. The selection of the Wright Cyclone was again found to be correct, as the engine possessed excellent growth potential, and helped cancel out the Fort's increasing growth in weight. The Wright company traced its origins directly back to the pioneering Wright brothers of Kitty Hawk fame, although it had experienced several structural and ownership changes by 1932, when a new version of the popular Cyclone – the F – was produced. The radial was made in large numbers throughout the 1930s, with ratings up to 900 hp at 2350 rpm on 91-octane fuel. The company knew that the versatile F had the potential for still further development, and this duly continued well past the magic 1000 hp mark with the G series of 1937. Production of the engine was in such demand for wartime B-17s that Studebaker built thousands under license.

The interior of the F held the vast majority of the changes. however, with over 400 modifications, additions and improvements having been made in light of combat experience. Modifications to the ball turret, landing gear, bomb racks, self-sealing oil tanks, ability to take 1100-gal 'Tokyo tanks' and improved electrical sources all contributed to make the B-17F a tough, combat-ready, bomber. Because many of these modifications and additions were incorporated on the production line, the B-17F was the first Fortress to use block numbers on the designation, denoting differences between batches of the same aeroplane. However, it should be noted that block numbers, (even if the same) used by Boeing, Douglas and Vega did not mean that the aircraft were similarly equipped. This led to considerable confusion when the bombers were being overhauled.

A visitor to Boeing examining a B-17F ready for roll out would find a fuselage of all-metal semi-monocoque construction, consisting of extruded angle section stringers and formed 'Z' section frames or formers, built on four longerons and covered with a stressed alclad skin. The fuselage was divided into five main compartments: nose compartment, pilots' cockpit, bomb bay, radio compartment and rear compartment.

The nose compartment accommodated the navigator-bombardier and was fitted with a plexiglass nose dome, with ball joint positions for machine guns, and a clear view panel for bomb aiming. The navigator's table and instruments were located on the port side of the compartment, the table having a compass recessed into the top surface protected by a hinged cover. A plexiglass dome was fitted into the upper structure for

RIGHT B-17Fs, with 42-5951 in the foreground, come together on Vega's Burbank production line. Vega production was laid out in a logical manner, with wing sections rolling down their own lines before being transferred to the fuselage for mating. Delivered to the USAAF in late May 1943, 42-5951 served with the Fifteenth Air Force in Italy, flying firstly with the 410th BS/301st BG, before being transferred to the 340th BS/97th BG. Nicknamed *Opissonya*, it was badly damaged by flak over Ploesti on 23 June 1944 and then downed by fighters a short while later. The bomber was being flown as a replacement aircraft by a crew from the 341st BS at the time, one of its crewmembers (Bombardier Lt David R Kingsley) winning a posthumous Medal of Honor for his bravery during the fateful sortie

FAR LEFT An early B-17F runs up its Cyclones at night on the Seattle ramp. As production increased, testing continued around the clock. The legend 'U.S. Army' under the wings was ordered to be eliminated, along with the red centre to the national insignia, on 15 May 1942

LEFT A Vega-built B-17F is seen on a test flight over a fog bank near Burbank. The instruction stencilling clearly stands out against the camouflage, while the national insignia carries the short-lived red surround. Note the clearly visible Norden bombsight in the clear plexiglass nose

LEFT A Douglas worker installs equipment in the bombardier's position. Note that the serial aft of the nose has been blocked out for 'security purposes'

RIGHT Vega-built B-17F 42-5886 is seen on a test flight from Burbank. Since Vega was very near Walt Disney's studio, many of the bombers received art work from company artists. Oddly, this was usually portrayed mid-fuselage (as seen here) rather than on the nose. Later nicknamed *The Jolly Roger*, this aircraft was shot down by fighters during the Schweinfurt raid of 17 August 1943 whilst flying with the 548th BS/385th BG. Of its ten-man crew, one evaded, three were made PoWs and six were killed

BELOW A steady stream of lead pours from the twin M-2 Brownings mounted in the Sperry ball turret during a night test at Boeing Field

astronomical navigation. This position was also fitted with ash trays, since crew members were allowed to smoke! Also, the compartment was sound insulated to a degree by the addition of a dark green padding applied over the internal structure.

Between the nose compartment and the front spar was situated the cockpit, this raised enclosure housing the pilot, co-pilot and a Sperry power turret, mounting two .50-cal machine guns. Both seats were adjustable for height, tilt and fore-and-aft movement, and armour plate protection was attached to the back of each. As with the nose compartment, this area was also insulated. The Sperry turret was located immediately behind the pilots' seats, and was operated from a standing position on a circular platform which revolved with the turret. Adjustable footrests on two vertical members could be used by the gunner if he was too short to operate the guns from the platform.

Between the main spars aft of the pilots' cockpit was the bomb bay, which was a heavily reinforced chamber that occupied a comparatively small plan area. Access to the radio compartment was provided by a walkway running centrally through the bomb bay supported by the vertical bomb channels, which were attached to the top of the fuselage.

The bulkheads at each end of the bomb bay were attached to the wing spars and, therefore, were heavily reinforced with

ABOVE An example of the mid-fuselage art applied at the Vega factory to a new B-17F

box-section members to carry the loads between the wings, as there was no actual wing structure in the fuselage itself.

The radio compartment was situated aft of the bomb bay and accommodated the radio operator on the port side. On the starboard side there was provision for two seats for extra crew members if carried. Over this compartment was a transparent removable hatch and provision for a machine gun, which slid along horizontal tracks from its stowage position between the inner skin of the fuselage and the top raised fairing, which terminated at the hatchway. The radio compartment was also fitted with sound-proofing insulation material.

The rear compartment accommodated the power-operated ball turret and the manually-operated twin gun position in the extreme tail. This installation mounted two .50-cal weapons sighted by a separate ring and bead sight which was connected by a linkage system to the mounting and moved in conjunction with the guns. The rear gunner operated in a kneeling position, but was supported by an adjustable seat to take the weight from his legs. Access to the rear gunner's position in flight was very restricted, and necessitated passing round the side of the retracted tail wheel. A small door was provided on the starboard side for use on the ground, or when a quick exit was desirable in the air. The two waist gun positions were fitted with windows which were opened by sliding forward a hand rail which automatically released them and pulled them clear of the openings.

Each wing was built in two main sections, comprising an inboard section, which carried the engine nacelles as an integral

Douglas employees swarm over one of the first B-17Fs to be assembled at Long Beach. Once again, the serial has been obscured on the nose, but note the war-time poster affixed above the pitot tube which states 'Give us the planes to deliver the goods'

Accompanied by a bit of a fanfare, B-17F 42-5705 (the first Vega-built Fort) is rolled out of its hangar. Lightnings, Venturas, C-47s, TWA DC-3s and a lone Boeing 247 fill the background. To underscore the productivity of Vega, this aircraft flew on 4 May 1942, which was six months ahead of the USAAF's schedule and one month ahead of the company's schedule! Vega would achieve the lowest man-hours required to build a Flying Fortress. This aircraft was retained for test and evaluation work by the USAAF following its delivery on 26 June 1942, only to be written off whilst based at Biggs AFB on 27 April 1943

part of the structure, and an outboard section to which was connected a detachable wing tip.

The wing was built up on two main spars, which were of strutted construction, the struts and booms being of box section and interconnected by fish-plate gussets. Each spar was attached to the fuselage by an upper and lower steel coupling and shear connection, with an intermediate subsidiary connection. In the inboard wing section, the ribs were also of strutted construction, employing box section struts between the spars and light tubular struts in the trailing edge. There were no stringers. Instead, the ribs were covered with a double skin, the inner layer being corrugated (the corrugations ran spanwise), and on top of this the surface skin was riveted. The outboard wing section was of similar construction to the inboard section, but the ribs were of tubular section throughout.

The fin was built in two sections, comprising a vertical section and a dorsal section, or extension. The vertical section was built up of two strutted spars with sheet metal ribs which had flanged lightening holes and were fluted laterally for extra stiffness. The fin was attached to the fuselage structure by two cou-

ABOVE Workers on scaffolding apply camouflage paint to the Boeing factory. Note the framework for the fake miniature 'city' that was erected atop the buildings

RIGHT A Boeing secretary enjoys a bit of sun atop one of the company's buildings that has been effectively camouflage – the fake houses to the right are a nice touch. However, little could be done to hide the runways

plings at the end of the spars, and was secured with two taper pins. The dorsal extension was built up of sheet metal vertical ribs and top-hat section stringers, covered by an alclad skin. The tailplane was also built up on two strutted spars with sheet metal ribs and top-hat section stringers, and was attached to the fuselage in a similar manner to the fin. All the control surfaces were metal, with fabric coverings. Both elevators pivoted on a common torque tube, which passed through the fuselage.

Each Wright Cyclone was mounted on welded steel tubular structures which were interchangeable for each engine, and had a four-point attachment to the fire walls which were, in turn, mounted on tubular structures secured to the front spar.

Each Cyclone was fitted with a B-2 exhaust-driven turbo-supercharger, control of which was obtained by automatic hydraulic regulators operated by cables from the cockpit. The regulators were in turn served by the engine oil pressure. The turbosuperchargers were incorporated in the engine exhaust duct recessed in the bottom of the engine nacelle and, when in operation, exhaust gases were discharged behind the super-chargers after turning the impellers.

ABOVE This late-model B-17F displays the enlarged nose windows, with a .50-cal machine gun and ammunition feed belts in place. Once both '.50s' were installed, the bombardier's area became quite cramped. The weapon was mounted as far forward as possible in an attempt to deter devastating Luftwaffe head-on attacks

LEFT Photographed on 25 November 1942, the prototype chin turret installation is seen on a late-model B-17F. This view also shows the gunner's control column to advantage

LEFT An underwing external bomb rack photographed at Douglas on 19 January 1943. The Long Beach factory would build 9439 wartime aircraft, including C-47s, Invaders and Flying Fortresses. Indeed, more aircraft were built at this facility than any other Douglas factory. When President Roosevelt called for 50,000 aircraft to be built a year on 16 May 1940, the Emergency Plant Facilities Program was created so that new factories could be built. Under this plan, the Long Beach facility would be financed by Douglas, with the government reimbursing the company over a period of five years and then assuming title to the facility

The throttle levers were located on the central console stand and could be operated with one hand, either individually, or the two inboard, the two outboard or the four together. The levers could be locked in any position and, if necessary, the two inboard only could be locked, leaving the outboard controls free to operate.

The mixture control levers could be set at four positions: Full Rich, Automatic Rich, Automatic Lean, and Idle Cut-off. Also, a friction damper device could be operated to retain the control levers in any position between Automatic Rich and Automatic Lean.

The engines were fitted with Hamilton Standard Hydromatic three-blade full-feathering propellers. Feathering and unfeathering was accomplished hydraulically by means of an electric motor-driven pump, mounted on the firewall of each nacelle. Engine oil, drawn from the oil line between the tank and engine inlet, was used in the pump when feathering. The oil was forced under pressure through the constant-speed governor to the propeller, where it overcame the constant-speed governing action and produced the feathering action. The feathering was controlled by a magnetic push button switch for each propeller. Each switch controlled a solenoid switch in the respective engine nacelle, which operated the electric engine-driven pump. The push button switches were held in the closed position, when pressed, by magnetic coils. When the propeller was completely feathered, the hydraulic pressure rapidly increased, and a pressure cut-out switch on the control head opened the magnetic coil circuit when the pressure reached 400-lb per square inch.

The 100-octane fuel was carried in six self-sealing tanks in the wings and two auxiliary tanks which could be installed in the bomb bay. Total capacity of the wing tanks was 1732-gal, and with the addition of the auxiliary bomb bay fuel tanks, the

BELOW Tail gun test set up for a Boeing B-17F at Seattle on 29 December 1941

total capacity could be increased to 2524-gal. Each Cyclone had its own system, the outboard radials being supplied by 437-gal tanks and the inboard engines by 215-gal tanks and 214-gal feeder tanks. The wing tanks were retained in cradles riveted to the spars, and were held against the upper wing surface by heavy straps under the tank shells. These straps were of heavy, formed alloy-channel section padded with neoprene and bolted to the wing structure at each end. The tanks consisted of self-sealing cells inside alloy shells, which had removable ends for inserting or withdrawing the cells.

For starting, take-off and high altitude, the engine-driven fuel pump of each system was assisted by a booster pump at the outlet of each fuel tank. These booster pumps were electrically-driven centrifugal pumps, and were capable of producing an additional 7-lb per square inch at the carburettor. For high altitude flying, they were necessary in order to prevent the vapourisation of the fuel before it reached the engine-driven pumps. No hand-operated pump was fitted.

A solenoid-operated shut-off valve was installed in each fuel line to permit the immediate stoppage of fuel flow, if that particular line was severed. The fuel could be transferred from one tank to another by a reversible, electrically-driven pump and selector valves.

Each Cyclone was equipped with a self-sealing oil tank,

With their fingers crossed, these Vega workers await the flight of a B-17F-1-VE – all have grown beards during the aircraft's construction due to the lack of spare time even for a shave! Note the Disney artwork above their heads

ABOVE A Vega inspector checks over the Hamilton Standard prop hub for any sign of defects prior to passing the bomber fit for delivery to the Army Air Force

ABOVE RIGHT As the war escalated, women began replacing more and more men at the production plants. After short, but extremely intensive, training courses, women were able to take over virtually every job on the B-17 production lines. These Vega employees are completing wiring on relay panels

RIGHT Boeing Flying Fortress workers share a laugh over a company poster stuck up on the bulletin board before heading back to the production line. Defence factories revolutionised the woman worker during the war, and resulted in massive social changes both in American home life and the economy

LEFT Building bombers wasn't an easy life, and these women are using all their collective muscle power to move hefty crates of B-17 components from the store to the production line at Seattle

BELOW A female worker delivers spark plugs to a mechanic preparing a B-17F for test flying. The Seattle ramp was swarming with activity during the day and most of the night, and rapid delivery of parts was essential in maintaining the flow of bombers to the USAAF. Note the Boeing fuel truck at the left of the photo

Flying low over the San Gabriel mountains, gleaming Vega-built B-17G 42-97991 undertakes its first shake down flight in early 1944. Of note are the various shades of aluminium that comprise its structure. In January 1944 the decision was made to eliminate camouflage paint starting with blocks G-35-BO, G-20-VE and G-35-DL. Assigned to the 366th BS/305th BG at Chelveston, in Northamptonshire, on 9 August 1944, this aircraft was lost to flak on the raid to Merseburg just 15 days later. Of its crew, led by Maj Von Turgeln, two were killed and nine captured

having a capacity of 45 gallons with an additional 5-gallon foaming space. An oil temperature regulator was installed in the outgoing line from each tank, directly behind an air inlet in the leading edge of the wing, adjacent to each nacelle. This regulator was equipped with a valve which by-passed the oil at very low temperatures, so that the oil cooler would not be damaged by an excess of pressure when the oil was in a cold, highly viscous state. The oil cooler shutters were controlled by a thermostatic valve, which was an integral part of the cooler. Being fully automatic, oil cooler controls were not necessary.

The tanks were equipped with an oil heat accelerator chamber, which was a cylindrical compartment extending between the tank inlet and outlet, and venting to the tank interior at each end so that the returning oil from the engine did not mix with the cold oil in the main interior of the tank. As the level of the hot oil fell, the cooler oil was brought into use, with the resultant rapid increase in the oil temperature.

For easier starting, an oil dilution system was incorporated whereby fuel was introduced into the oil at the end of a flight, thus thinning the oil and preventing it from congealing as it cooled down. When the engine was restarted, heat rapidly evaporated the fuel and left the oil warm and free flowing.

The B-17's flying controls were quite conventional, the primary controls consisting of rudder pedals, an elevator control column and aileron control wheel fitted to both the pilot's and co-pilot's positions. The rudder pedals were pivoted on a transverse shaft, which was common to both sets, and operated the rudder torque tube by means of cables. The elevator control columns were of tubular construction, inside which were the cables from the aileron hand wheel, which operated the geared mechanisms of the ailerons. The elevators were operated at the torque tube by cables connected to the control columns.

Trim tab controls were also installed. The aileron tab was operated by a knob, which turned the cable-controlled tab actuating screw. Both the rudder and elevator trim tabs were operated by hand wheels on the same principle as the aileron tab control. Approximately six or seven turns of the hand wheels were necessary to cover the full travel of the tabs.

The hydraulic system operated the cowl flaps and the brakes. Normally, pressure was supplied by two Pesco engine-driven pumps, with a capacity of three gallons per minute at normal cruising speed and 800 lb per square inch pressure. The pumps built up pressure in the accumulator to 750 lb per square inch, at which pressure a regulator unloaded the pumps and bypassed their output back to the tank. The pressure stored in the accumulator was used to operate the hydraulic mechanisms until it fell to 600 lb per square inch, when the regulator redirected the pump output back into the system. When the accumulator pressure again reached 750 lb per square inch the cycle was repeated.

The emergency hand pump was used for two functions – either to store pressure in the accumulator (if the engine-driven pumps were either put out of action, or the port engines were not running), or to provide pressure to operate the hydraulic mechanisms direct.

All three units of the landing gear were retractable and were operated by electric motors. The main units were installed beneath each inboard nacelle and retracted forward, the wheels projecting slightly below the contour of the nacelles. They consisted of a single, cantilever type oleo, with a torsion link, a retracting strut and a forked drag strut, and were of tubular construction.

An electric motor in each nacelle operated the retracting strut, which consisted of an outer casing, inside which a tubular extension, connected to the drag strut, moved up and down by means of a screw system, turned by the electric motor. The torsion link was installed to transmit the torque from the cantilever wheel axle to the landing gear leg, and thus keep the wheel in alignment.

The tailwheel was of the single oleo, cantilever type, consisting of the wheel assembly, a pivoting assembly, to which the wheel was attached, a floating oleo strut, connected to the pivoting assembly and also a retracting unit. The retracting unit

A Vega worker is seen installing wiring prior to the attachment of the tail gun position, which was built as a separate component

Seemingly never-ending B-17G wing sections head down the Vega production line

was electrically operated on a similar principle to the main landing gear units. The tailwheel retracted fully into the fuselage.

The bomb bay was closed by two doors, operated electrically by a system of motor-driven actuating screws hinged at each side on the main compression struts of the structure. For emergency operation, a direct mechanical system disconnected the motor-driven mechanism and operated the doors.

On the port door, a mechanical lock prevented the use of the bomb release mechanism until the doors were in the fully open position. As a further precaution, a safety switch (also on the port door) prevented the electrical circuit from operating until the doors were open. The doors were operated by the bombardier, the operating handle having a lug so positioned that when the handle was in the closed position, the release lever could not be moved out of the safe position.

The wing flaps were of the split trailing edge type, and were also operated by an electrically-driven retracting screw, which drove a series of five actuating struts along the length of each

LEFT Interior framing on a B-17G plexiglass nose cone is installed while the exterior is polished on the Douglas line. A great deal of care was taken to make sure that the unit was not scratched during the production process

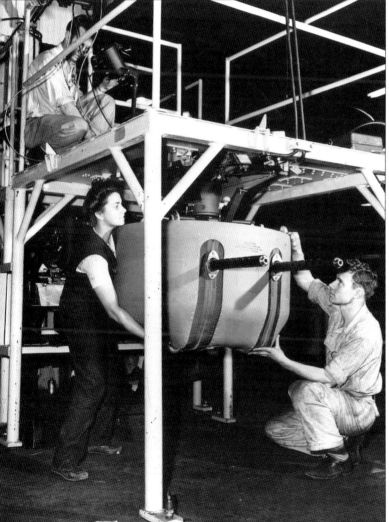

LEFT Workers prepare to move a chin turret for installation on a Boeing B-17G. Note the individual with the turret control mechanism atop the jig, who gave the unit one final check before the turret was installed in an aircraft

BELOW Sometimes workers had to get inside the wing, as seen here, whilst riveting was taking place. The female worker in the wing is wearing a popular piece of patriotic wartime jewellry – a pin depicting a sailor

flap, at the hinges. An emergency, manually-operated system, of the hand-crank type, was also provided.

A low pressure oxygen system was installed, operating at a maximum of 400 lb per square inch. The oxygen was stored in twenty bottles, eight being located behind the pilot's seat, seven below the pilot's floor and three beneath the radio compartment floor. An auxiliary bottle was installed in both power turrets.

Each of the 18 main bottles had a duration of approximately five hours at 30,000 ft. Thus, with a nominal crew of six, the oxygen system had a duration of approximately 15 hours at 30,000 ft. Eleven regulators were installed at various crew positions, and check valves were incorporated at each bottle outlet to prevent the loss of pressure to the whole system should one be destroyed.

As can be seen, the B-17F was a complex, but logically designed, aircraft that offered its crew a great deal of structural safety – something that would be needed as the air war against Germany intensified.

As previously mentioned, production responsibility for the

ABOVE A Boeing worker rivets on a long line of tail gun positions. Note the suitably stylised company uniform

RIGHT A female crane operator carefully manoeuvres a wing section so that it can be attached to a Vega-built B-17G

Wright made sure that the flow of R-1820s to the BVD (Boeing, Vega, Douglas) Pool was constant. Once at the factory, the engines would be thoroughly inspected before being fitted to the wing assemblies – an activity being undertaken here by this Vega employee

aircraft was split between the three companies. Vega really set the pace by delivering its first B-17F-1-VE (42-5705) six months ahead of schedule, and by eventually achieving the lowest man-hours per aircraft of any of the companies.

Douglas Aircraft in Long Beach also set up for production of the B-17F-DL with the same sort of assistance from Boeing as received by Vega. Douglas block production went from 1-DL to 80-DL and saw 600 B-17F-DLs were built before production switched over to the G-model. Each company had constructed its B-17s with minor differences, and such variations could be seen in the nose armament – the number of guns being installed in this position varied between companies and production blocks. The phasing-in of Douglas and Vega into Fortress production went fairly smoothly, and greatly increased the flow of aircraft to the combat fronts. Interestingly, the first B-17F was completed by Vega on 4 May 1942, the first by Boeing on 30 May and the first by Douglas on 9 June.

How much did a B-17F cost? Only Vega had a fixed price contract which set the cost at $337,025 per bomber – Boeing and Douglas had contracts of escalating scale. Boeing had originally (and often incorrectly) figured the profit into the final figure, but the new contract allowed the company a six per cent profit over cost of the aircraft, although this was later reduced to five per cent. However, as more items and better equipment was added to the production line, the cost of each aircraft fluctuated, and the price of B-17F could run between $310,000 to $402,000.

The B-17F's fuel capacity increased from 2550 to 3630 gallons during the type's production run, while its bomb load could also be increased to 17,600 lbs for very short missions. This was achieved through the addition of external bomb racks under the wings which could accommodate 4000 lbs (these wing racks were fitted to the B-17F-20 to -50-VE, F-30 to F-130-BO and F-20 to F-65-DL). It was not all that common for groups to utilise the external racks for combat missions, however. All of the 2300 F-models built by Boeing, 500 by Vega and 605 by Douglas were delivered in Olive Drab and Neutral Grey camouflage.

USAAF thinking about strategic bombing had solidified fairly well by the time the B-17F was introduced to active service. Neither the USAAF or the RAF had, at that stage, counted on the ferocious resistance that would be provided by the Luftwaffe for most of the war. The cover of darkness for RAF bombers also concealed an increasingly effective German night-fighter force which slaughtered Lancasters, Stirlings and Halifaxes with equal zeal.

As mentioned, the first B-17E raid on 17 August 1942 saw 12 aircraft of the 97th BG head off to the rail yards at Rouen-Sotteville for a first strike on enemy targets. The formation, which also included Brig-Gen Ira Eaker, was covered by RAF Spitfires. The target was reached, attacked and the returning forces landed in Britain without loss. It seemed almost easy. The next ten missions saw the loss of just two E-models, which was certainly acceptable attrition considering the condition of the war. Certain Allied commanders noticed how well the Eighth Air Force seemed to being doing, and many senior men felt that maybe they had hit on something big with this 'daylight precision bombing stuff'. However, history has a way of quickly changing events, and a good portion of the Eighth's small bomber force was quickly transferred to North Africa in late 1942 when Rommel's *Afrika Korps* began to stall the Allied advance. This gave the Luftwaffe in Western Europe time to think about the Eighth, its Flying Fortresses and its tactics.

The arrival of the F-model enabled the Eighth to begin increased operations against the Continent, starting with short range missions to develop tactics and gain experience. Formation flying in defensive boxes was no easy task for young pilots just awarded their wings (each combat box usually consisted of 18 aircraft, with two or three boxes positioned more or less vertically to form a combat wing – many wings would quite often form a single bomber stream for a strike against the enemy). Mid-air collisions were, unfortunately, not uncommon, especially as aircraft left or arrived back at their bases during the

With the use of a fork lift, completed outer wing panels head for the Boeing assembly line

murky British weather – weather which was totally unlike the sunshine and clear air at most American training bases. Once the formations were in the air, they were an awe-inspiring sight – even in the early days of America's involvement.

However, short-range British fighters were only able to escort the bombers part way to the target. The longer-range American fighters such as the P-47 Thunderbolt, P-38 Lightning and P-51 Mustang were starting to arrive in small numbers, but still needed developing before their escort potential could be fully realised. The commanders of the Eighth hoped the defensive fire power of the boxes would be enough to discourage the Luftwaffe when the bombers finally ventured deep into Germany. It wasn't.

New American bases in Britain saw more and more Fortresses arriving. Most of these aircraft spent their brief lives parked outside, and new problems arose as the damp English weather began to creep into every crevice of the Fort, causing everything from accelerated turbo failures to runaway engines. These problems were maddening for the crew chiefs, who had to trace down each defect and attempt to find a cure. A large body of maintenance literature and procedures was created

RIGHT Under camouflage netting at the Long Beach plant, B-17G rear fuselages receive work on their Cheyenne tail turrets – note the large slabs of silver-painted armour plate attached to the sides of the units. Photographed on 29 August 1944, Lois McFarland, Gladys Roley, Elaine Bradfield and Goldie Roach are doing their part to ensure the constant flow of bombers to the European fighting fronts

BELOW Rudder control installations are worked on as B-17G fuselages head down the production line

LEFT A Vega employee works on the hub of the massive US Royal tyre and wheel assembly prior to installing the unit on the B-17G in the background. Note how this aircraft has camouflaged cowlings

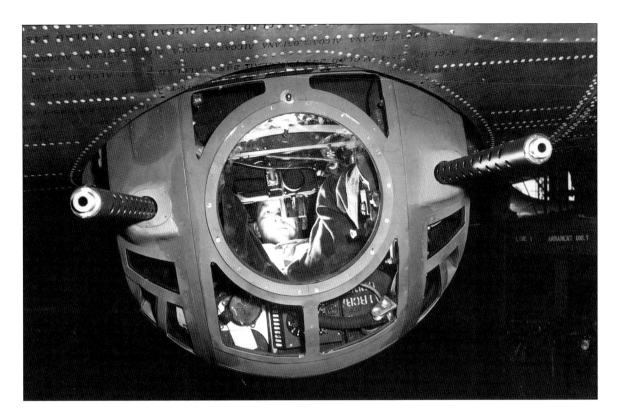

from this search and repair process so new maintenance crews could be thoroughly briefed upon their arrival in Britain.

With just four B-17F bomb groups (the 91st, 303rd, 305th and 306th) and approximately 200 aircraft in Britain at the start of 1943, the bombing component of the Eighth was not all that 'mighty' since so many of the Forts had been ordered to North Africa. Operations did increase through foul weather, however, with targets in France and the Low Countries hit – RAF Spitfires escorted these raids. U-Boat pens were singled out for particular attention, and regular 'visits' were made to Brest and St Nazaire. During these attacks, the Americans found that the Germans had developed a new, and frighteningly effective, tactic.

Wary of the B-17's heavy armament, the Luftwaffe decided to broach the bombers weak point – its nose. The Bf 109s and Fw 190s would attack the bombers head-on, and with closing speeds well in excess of 500 mph, the chances of a mid-air collision were great. Such attacks allowed the fighter pilots to bring their cannon and machine guns to bear on the pilots' compartment (unarmed against frontal attack) without the fear of being counted by a 'wall of lead'. Indeed, only a single weapon was mounted in the plexiglass nose, and this could be bolstered by the twin '.50s' in the top turret if required.

The Forts still managed to get to their targets, but the results were far from impressive. The U-Boat pens were made of extremely thick reinforced-concrete, which the B-17s' bombs could not effectively penetrate. On 27 January 1943, the 306th

ABOVE A Boeing technician performs final checks on the Sperry ball turret as a B-17G rolls down the line

RIGHT
Bombardier's compartment in Boeing-built B-17G 42-31150 on 21 September 1943. Note how the mechanism for controlling and firing the chin turret is stowed to the right in this cramped position. The large panel mounted on the top right fuselage illustrated the different types of bombs that could be carried in the bomb bay, along with B-17G climb and glide angle information. Once completed, this particular bomber was issued to the 332nd BS/94th BG at Rougham, in Norfolk, on 15 October 1943. Nicknamed *Wonga Wonga*, it was subsequently written off in a crash-landing at Debach airfield, in Suffolk, on 22 February 1944

LEFT Looking to the rear in B-17G 42-102383 on 23 February 1944. This view shows the new staggered waist gun positions which use the K-6 enclosed waist gun mount. Flexible ammunition belts were fed from wooden boxes attached to the sides of the fuselage, while the large curved piece of metal extending from the gun mount to the floor was armour plating. A wooden door led to the extreme rear fuselage. The ball turret was wrapped with a wooden ring, while a small wood door in the floor allowed the gunner, or another crew member, to attempt to clean the turret viewing panels in flight

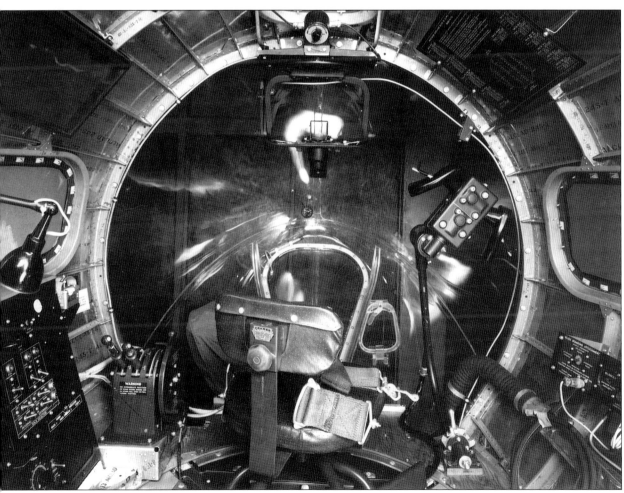

Detail view of a waist gunner's position on B-17G 42-31264 on 5 October 1943, showing the early style window opening and the .50-cal weapon affixed to an E-8 recoil mount. Note the wooden ammunition box at the extreme left. This bomber was delivered to the AAF in October 1943, and spent its entire life with base training units in Nevada. It was eventually passed to the Reclamation Finance Center (RFC) at Walnut Ridge, in Arkansas, on 11 January 1946 and subsequently scrapped

BG made the first B-17F raid on German soil when its Forts attacked Wilhelmshaven. Head-on attacks continued with deadly results, causing groups to effect modifications to the plexiglass nose 'in the field', which saw more weapons fitted. However, these proved to be of little use as the 'plexi' fractured under the strain of the extra ordnance. Hasty and crude modifications were therefore undertaken to brace the structure, while ball and socket mounts were installed in the nose windows immediately aft of the plexiglass nose cone, and single .50-cals fitted at an angle so as to fire forward as much as possible.

As the bombers continued their attacks into Europe, Eighth commanders were still pleasantly surprised at just how low their losses were. The Germans were certainly pressing home attacks, but the loss rate of B-17Fs was well below the acceptable 'ten per cent' figure the AAF felt they could bear (B-17 crews had their own thoughts on just how 'acceptable' this loss rate was).

By May 1943 the bomber force was rapidly building, with five new bomb groups now active – the 94th, 95th, 96th, 351st and 379th – and extended range P-47Cs, fitted with drop tanks to slake the thirst of their Pratt & Whitney R-2800s, now available to escort the bombers deeper into enemy territory. The raids began to increase greatly but around the middle of the year a new trend was noticed – losses were beginning to mount.

The fact that more aircraft were attacking hostile targets inevitably meant that there would be proportionally more losses, but the rate was rapidly nearing the 'ten per cent' figure – the Luftwaffe was finally starting to make its presence felt. At this time, there were around 600 B-17Fs in Britain, and the Eighth decided to mount a 'Blitz Week', with bombers attacking as many targets as possible, including the now-familiar submarine pens and aircraft factories. Three-hundred Forts attacked Fw 190 plants on 28 July, these raids seeing the deepest penetration into Germany to date. However, 22 of the bombers

On the sign in the image:

DEPARTMENT 12 LEADS
HERE'S ONE FOR MacARTHUR
2 WEEKS AHEAD OF SCHEDULE

A wing section heads down the line adorned with a typically patriotic slogan which urged the workers to speed up production

failed to return, along with their 220 crew members. A P-47 escort kept losses lower than they probably could have been, but this was still a high figure. Raids continued on the 29th and 30th against military and industrial targets, escorting Thunderbolts attacking wave after wave of fighters. The 'Blitz Week' saw the loss of no fewer than 128 B-17Fs in combat and associated accidents, resulting in what the AAF 'brass' considered to be an acceptable temporary loss rate of over 20 per cent! This was certainly not acceptable to the bomber crews, however.

Despite these losses, more ambitious raids were scheduled for August. It was planned to send the largest B-17 force yet assembled to bomb Schweinfurt and Regensburg on 17 August, but bad weather delayed part of the force from taking off and the bombers went over the targets in two groups, their defensive power thus reduced. The Germans, knowing that escorting fighters could not come this far, were 'waiting for the kill' in large numbers, and no fewer than 60 Forts were knocked out of the sky. Due to the distance to the target, the B-17s continued on to North Africa, where the numbed survivors could count their losses. This mission had suffered a 19 per cent loss rate.

The Forts ventured out over another heavily defended target on 6 September when 300 aircraft attacked Stuttgart. Bad weather separated some of the formations, so the Luftwaffe could again concentrate on smaller, less well-defended, groups – 45 B-17Fs were knocked down.

During October 1943, the AAF undertook another 'Blitz Week', and Fortresses visiting targets in Germany and Poland – Schweinfurt was hit again. This time the German fighters intercepted early, forcing escorting Thunderbolts to jettison their external fuel tanks, and thus reducing their range. Pulling back until the Thunderbolts finally had to turn home for England, the fighters roared into the bomber formation, hitting the lead and low groups in a new battle plan which immediately paid off – 28 bombers were knocked down before the formations even reached the target. By the time the mission to destroy the ball bearing factories was over, 60 Forts had been shot down, while five others crashed back at base.

Losses such as this would clearly decimate the Eighth if they were allowed to continue. The loss rate also did nothing for crew morale, many men feeling that they were being sent on suicide missions that were inflicting no permanent damage on

The instrument panel, finished in black, of a Boeing-built B-17G, photographed on 9 February 1944

the enemy. Clearly, the Flying Fortress would once again have to be improved, while the need for long-range escort fighters was nothing short of desperate.

By the time the last B-17F rolled off the tri-company production lines, it was a different aircraft from the very first F-model. Modifications had been incorporated into the airframe to boost performance, increase efficiency and add armament. Around 100 of the last bombers to leave the Douglas production line in Long Beach were, for all intents and purposes, the first of the new B-17Gs, since they incorporated chin turrets and some of the modifications which would be carried by actual fully-blown G-models – to simplify records, the Eighth Air Force would categorise any Fortress with a chin turret as a B-17G.

The G-model was the ultimate Flying Fortress, truly living up to its public relations-image name, and it was also the last production model. Extra armour plate, guns and ammunition, plus a variety of new internal equipment, increased the bomber's weight by two tons, with a corresponding decrease in performance. And although the G-model was stressed to accommodate a bomb load of up to 20,000 lbs, its small bomb bay (about the same size as a medium bomber's – the Lancaster could carry a much greater payload) would not allow this to be physically carried. Indeed, the modest dimensions of the B-17's bomb bay was one of the RAF's chief criticisms of the type. In order to make up this shortfall, the aircraft's wings were stressed for external racks to carry extra bombs.

The forward fuselage of the first production run of G-models looked very similar to the B-17F, but one of the distinguishing features soon added to the production line were the bowed

Douglas employees pose with a B-17G which was 'donated' to the USAAF by funds raised among factory workers. Note the chalked name *PISTOL PACKIN' MAMA* under the slogan – one of at least 16 Forts to receive this sobriquet

The cavernous Boeing factory is
filled with the din of non-stop
riveting as G-model rear fuselages
are assembled

nose windows, which housed a .50-cal apiece. This type of installation meant the gunner could get a much better angle of fire – quite a few of these windows were installed at combat depots rather than on the production line.

Early production B-17Gs had waist gun positions similar to the F-model in that they were directly opposite each other. However, in combat this proved rather impractical, and made conditions cramped as the gunners tried to swing their heavy weapons in the rarefied heights. The gunners were, however, better protected from the freezing temperatures in the B-17G through the fitment of a fixed window over their positions. Although this did slightly restrict visibility, it certainly made their difficult lives that much easier. Later production G-models had the side gunner positions staggered so they would have more room at their stations. As the war progressed, many Fortress missions were flown with just one waist gunner as Luftwaffe formations became depleted. The waist positions also had large wooden boxes installed to hold greater quantities of ammunition, thus reducing the amount of time the gunners had to spend re-supplying their weapons.

Another improvement was the Cheyenne tail turret, which was developed at the United Airlines Modification Center in Cheyenne, Wyoming. The new turret reduced fuselage length by five inches and gave the tail gunner a better weapons system with which to work, while making his cramped space more user-friendly. A bicycle style seat was installed so the gunner would not have to remain sat for long periods in the uncomfortable kneeling position. The primitive ring and bead sight was also replaced with a reflector sight, and wooden boxes holding 500 rounds of ammo for each gun were installed. The position's plexiglass area was also increased to give better visibility.

United shipped many of these turrets directly overseas, where they were installed on arriving G-models, and the unit was also quickly incorporated into the production lines.

The first B-17G (still retaining the designation Model 299-O) flew from Seattle on 21 May 1943, but the first aircraft to be delivered to the AAF came from Douglas, and this event occurred on 4 September of the same year. The G-model was armed with 13 .50-cal machine guns, carrying a total of 6400 rounds of ammunition. Some 8680 B-17Gs were built, with Douglas responsible for 2395 and Vega 2250. Fortress production stopped altogether on 13 April 1945.

Britain purchased B-17Gs as the Fortress III, some 85 being bought and subsequently fitted with radar for use by Coastal Command and two RAF Pathfinder units.

Indeed, the bulk of the B-17Gs built were flown across the Atlantic to Britain, where they were swiftly issued to USAAF bomb groups in East Anglia – by February 1944 the type outnumbered the F-model in the Eighth Air Force inventory. The Fifteenth Air Force in Italy also began receiving G-models in late 1943, but they had to soldier on with their B-17Fs for a longer period, since the Eighth had priority on new Fortresses. The fighting in southern Europe was just as hard and just as deadly for the crews of the Fifteenth's bomb groups, although they got nowhere near the publicity the 'Mighty Eighth' received.

Various forms of radar and improved navigation devices also began appearing in B-17Gs in 1944, making the type even more accurate in locating and destroying enemy targets.

The first bomb group in the England to receive the G-model was the 401st, with the 447th, 452nd and 457th quickly following suit. By this stage in the war the Eighth had established a policy of converting all its four-engined bomb groups to the B-17, meaning the B-24 Liberators of the 34th, 486th, 487th, 490th and 493rd BG all had to be replaced by the 'new' Boeing bomber. By this time, the P-51 Mustang was coming into service, and it was able to escort the Forts on their deepest raids, effectively wiping aside the remaining Luftwaffe threat.

'Thousand Bomber' raids became the order of the day as all 12 Eighth Air Force bomb groups sent aircraft to attack enemy targets. These huge formations were inspiring sights, taking half an hour to pass over any given point – thus gaining for themselves the nickname 'aluminium overcast'. Despite all the advent of long-range fighters and better B-17s, the tough targets still remained tough. During March 1944, the Eighth visited Berlin and lost 69 B-17s – the highest loss rate suffered by VIII Bomber Command during the war. The Germans had perfected the accuracy of their flak batteries, and new weapons like unguided rockets and the Me 262 jet fighter and Me 163 rocket-powered interceptor were also making their presence felt. Despite this, the Germans still failed to turn back a single raid.

By April 1944, the Eighth could muster 1000 B-17Gs, but by August there would be almost 2000 – figures so high that there was no hope of the enemy doing enough damage to the bombers to prevent its major industrial centres and cities from being destroyed. By VE-Day, 2300 B-17Gs were based in Britain, and another 500 were with the Fifteenth in Italy.

With the advent of D-Day on 6 June 1944, B-17 missions switched to attacks on positions in France and the Low Countries. Any sort of military target was hit: Rail lines were slashed, airfields uprooted, dams breached and supply depots demolished. The Eighth, with its B-17Gs, had became a mighty juggernaut steamrollering across Hitler's 1000-year *Reich*, thus bringing hope to the imprisoned millions of occupied Europe.

A steel net was beginning to close around Germany as the Luftwaffe was decimated, and vital war industries and fuel sources were destroyed. Even the technologically-advanced V-weapons were not invulnerable. Launching sites for the V1 and V2 were hit hard, and regularly, reducing the terrible effect of these weapons upon Britain and the Low Countries.

As the 1944 ground on, the Americans increased pressure for shuttle raids to be flown whereby distant German targets would be hit – the B-17Gs would continue on to the USSR for

re-supply and refuelling, since the range to the target was so great that return was not possible in one flight. The Eighth participated in its first shuttle mission on 21 June 1944, bombing assigned targets and then landing at the Soviet base at Poltava. The Luftwaffe marked the occasion of this first mission with a surprise raid on the communist airfield, destroying 69 Forts on the ground, igniting a fuel storage area and setting off bomb dumps – many more aircraft were heavily damaged. The Soviets did not like the idea of having US aircraft flying over their territory, so the shuttle flights were abandoned shortly thereafter.

As the war began to grind to an end, the high command figured that bomber crews had a better chance of survival, so the number of missions they were required to fly to complete a tour was increased – the famous 'Catch-22. The required mission tally went from 25 to 30 and, finally, to 35 – by which time even the most hardened crew must have had very frayed nerves.

The Germans were hardy opponents – it took 291,508 B-17 missions dropping 640,036 tons of bombs to bring final victory in Europe. It also cost the lives of over 45,000 Eighth Air Force crewmen. To say that the Flying Fortress was an essential instrument in Hitler's defeat would certainly be an understatement.

Stacks of assembled formers and longerons await installation in Fortress fuselage sections at the Douglas plant in early1943. The tail section nearest the camera was soon mated with its remaining 'body parts' to form B-17F 42-5870, which went on to see much action with the Fifteenth Air Force in 1943/44, serving firstly with the 49th BS/2nd BG, followed by the 419th BS/301st BG. Relegated to the role of weather aircraft in late April 1944, the veteran bomber eventually returned to the USA exactly one year later and was duly scrapped the following August

CHAPTER 5

FORT WITH A DIFFERENCE

THE STANDARD B-17E was powered by four Wright R-1820-65 radials, which were fine, trustworthy, engines, but they only developed 1200 hp apiece at 25,000 ft – the B-17E's flight manual listed a rather optimistic top speed of 317 mph at that altitude. Vega was quite creative in coming up with new ideas for the tried and true airframe, and the company decided to undertake a project to increase the bomber's performance.

Vega Model V-143 was a paper design which mated the B-17 with four of the new, and massive, Wright R-3350 radials, while the V-144 had the Pratt & Whitney R-4360 Wasp Major as its powerplant – both engines pumped out 3000 hp. Perhaps these designs were not overly practical, but they were pointing the way towards an interesting idea that *did* come to fruition.

The Vega Model V-134-1 was submitted to the military as a proposed new-build Flying Fortress equipped with four sleek Allison V-1710-89 V-12 inlines, each developing 1425 hp. This was an overall increase of 900 hp, and the sleek cowlings around the V-12s would also improve streamlining and add a further boost to performance. Lockheed and Vega had had plenty of experience with this engine, since the Allison-powered P-38 Lightning was then in full-scale production at Burbank.

As the Flying Fortress was designed and built around air-cooled motors, the wing of the V-134-1 would need to be redesigned to accommodate the complexity of plumbing required for the various radiators of the liquid-cooled engines.

The USAAF liked the 'paper plane', and initially agreed to let Vega build a new aircraft with the serial 42-73515 (negotiations for the new design had started on 4 March 1942, and a contract was signed on 10 July of the same year), but somewhere along the line it was decided to utilise Boeing-built B-17E 41-2401. The reason for this change has been lost to time, but the aircraft was probably surplus to requirements, and it would save time to modify an existing airframe, rather than to build an entirely new one. Accordingly, the B-17E was pulled into a Burbank hangar (interestingly, this was the same airframe that had initially been transferred to Vega for use as a pattern aircraft when that company was setting up its license-built B-17F production line at the southern California airfield). The modified aircraft received the USAAF designation XB-38.

The wing was de-mated from the fuselage and work began on installing the plumbing, radiators, oil coolers and other equipment necessary for the operation of the Allisons. To make the E-model more like a B-17F, its Bendix belly turret was replaced with a mock-up of a Sperry unit. The radiators were installed in the wing leading edge, and large openings were cut to provide plenty of cooling air.

The Allison motor mounts were installed to hold the V-12s, and their three-bladed propellers, on modified firewalls. The interior of the fuselage was rigged to hold a variety of test instruments, and oil coolers were located in the under portion of each cowling – sleek, handmade, units that wrapped tightly around the V-12s. Otherwise, the majority of the airframe was stock B-17E, with the top turret and tail gun being retained, as were the side gunners' positions.

At first, work proceeded smoothly, but it soon became intermittent as employees were pulled off the new design to work on other vital projects. It was not until May 1943 that the XB-38 was ready for its flight testing.

After thorough ground checks, the all natural metal prototype lifted off from the Burbank runway for the first time on 19 May 1943 with pilot Bud Martin and co-pilot George MacDonald at the controls. Calculations showed that the XB-38 would be 30 to 50 mph faster than a standard F-model, which was a significant increase in performance. Ground runs had also indicated that the Allisons could develop full power in their new installations, and the first five flights went very well, with lots of data being gathered on engine operation and efficiency.

The XB-38 was grounded after its sixth flight when the

The XB-38 in flight over the San Gabriel Mountains near Burbank. Note how the hand-made cowlings for the Allisons neatly blend into the circular firewalls originally intended for the Wright radial engines

exhaust manifold joints began giving way – a situation that could have resulted in a serious fire had they failed completely. Once repair and modification work had been carried out on the manifolds the flight programme resumed, but disaster struck on the ninth test hop.

Martin and MacDonald departed Burbank on 16 June 1943 and, at first, it appeared the test flight would be entirely normal. However, shortly into the scheduled test programme, a serious fire developed in the number three Allison. Martin reached forward and pulled the red fire extinguisher handles for number

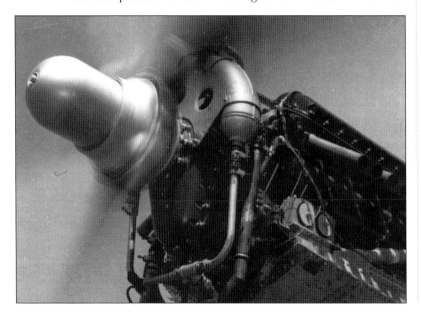

ABOVE The XB-38 is towed out of the experimental hangar for the installation of the outer wing panels and three-bladed propellers. At this point the armament has not been added, nor has the serial been painted on the vertical tail. Note the 'XB38' legend applied behind the pilots' station and the large wing openings for the Allisons' radiators. Oil coolers for the V-12s were located under the engine, the openings providing air

LEFT Using a section of discarded Flying Fortress wing, Vega built a test cell so that the Allison could be fully tested in its new 'home'

three on the instrument panel. This unleashed a torrent of chemicals inside the cowling, which would hopefully smother the fire being fed by the airflow blasting through the nacelle. However, the flames would not extinguish, and their continual fanning by the airflow saw them start to 'eat back' into the aluminium towards the main wing fuel tank.

The pilots realised that disaster was just moments away. Martin pointed the stricken bomber toward uninhabited territory and activated the auto pilot, allowing the two pilots to rapidly unstrap their seat belts and jump from the main crew entrance hatch. In a very unusual stroke of bad luck, both their parachutes malfunctioned, MacDonald being killed in the fall while Martin was critically injured. As the fire increased, the XB-38 fell off on one wing and dove into the floor of the San Fernando, being totally destroyed in the ensuing explosion.

Even though the XB-38 had been demolished, Vega and the AAF proceeded with the Model V-140 – this aircraft was to be an interesting combination of the XB-38, XB-40 and B-17F. The Allison-powered V-140 was to carry the standard bomb load of the F-model, but was to be equipped with the extra armament of the XB-40 'fighter' so it could also act in the escort role!

The V-140 was to take the place of the standard B-17Fs being built at Burbank, but the programme was personally cancelled by Gen Henry 'Hap' Arnold, who felt that the supplies of the R-1820 would remain adequate till war's end. Arnold must also have had doubts on the overall performance of the dual-mission V-140, and the design was allowed to quietly disappear as Vega churned out thousands of B-17Fs that fought their way to victory on every war front.

This evocative wartime view shows the XB-38 being refuelled under acres of camouflage netting at Burbank. Note the many false trees that formed part of the plant's extensive camouflage. During the XB-38's short life, the natural metal cowlings received a coat of aluminium paint and the spinners were finished in red. Note the early type B-17E top turret and two extra pitot tubes, fitted for the test programme, just visible behind and above the bombardier's position. Sadly, the XB-38 was destroyed before enough flight data could be gathered to quantify the type's performance

CHAPTER 6 SPIRIT OF BOEING

AMERICAN AIRCRAFT manufacturers have often made special use of particular production aircraft – aircraft that perhaps marked a production milestone, or commemorated a special event. One such aircraft was B-17G-70-BO 43-37716, which was Boeing's 5000th Flying Fortress built since the Japanese surprise attack on Hawaii on 7 December 1941. Realising that a great deal of publicity and patriotic zeal could be garnered by commemorating that bomber in some special manner was not lost upon Boeing. Accordingly, it was decided to let all of Boeing's 'Ralph and Rosie the Riveters' paint their signatures on the aircraft as it rolled down the production line towards completion.

Actually, this was not a bad idea, as it served as a further bond between workers, many of whom had travelled from across the USA to find fruitful employment at Boeing. It must be remembered that America was still recovering from the effects of the Great Depression at the time, and the chance for a job with a good wage stood out like a beacon in a dark night.

The zeal with which the workers wielded their paint brushes probably came as a surprise to Boeing officials, and even component parts were arriving at the factory plastered with names scribbled on in multi-colour paints. As the aircraft came together, it gathered not only local press but national coverage in magazines and newspapers across the country – often in conjunction with selling more war bonds.

The aircraft was given the obvious name of *5 GRAND*, and there was almost a party atmosphere among production line workers as each sector was allowed to paint their signatures or messages on the shining alclad skin. Some Boeing press releases from the time refer to the aircraft as the 'Easter Egg' due to its combination of colours.

The aircraft was extensively photographed as it came together, moving down the line with more and more signatures being added. When it came time to roll the nearly complete bomber out of the production hangar, it was decided to have Boeing workers manually push the four-engined warrior through the open doors, resulting in yet another great 'photo op', with its attendant patriotic publicity.

Once on the flight test line, final equipment was added and engine runs were undertaken. *5 GRAND* was the subject of an elaborate dedication ceremony when it was officially handed over to the USAAF in May 1944, a bottle of champagne being broken over a chunk of armour plate fitted between the twin .50-cal Brownings in the chin turret.

The picking of the crew for *5 GRAND* even achieved publicity, the USAAF making sure that a 'home town boy' was chosen as its pilot – Edward Collins Unger was from Seattle, and he duly 'picked' a co-pilot from the same city. Also, period USAAF and Boeing press releases stressed that Unger chose 'an all-bachelor crew', since the pilot supposedly claimed that bachelors could make a complete commitment to combat compared to married men.

By the time the crew picked up *5 GRAND* at a combat depot in Kearney, Nebraska, on 30 June 1944 for the ferry flight to

This photograph perhaps best symbolises the spirit of Boeing. Hundreds of workers surround *5 GRAND* prior to the aircraft's roll-out, while other Forts near completion in the background. Note the 'Let's Get 'em Flying!' banner in the background

Great Britain, the bomber had more than 35,000 signatures and messages splashed across its skin. At this point, some thought was given to stripping the metal of all signatures, since it was a distinct possibility that the Luftwaffe would make a special effort to destroy this aircraft, since the resulting publicity would be great for the Nazis. However, it was decided that the names would stay.

On the flight to Great Britain, Unger and his crew discovered that the aircraft was about seven miles per hour slower that a standard natural-metal B-17G. This was due, of course, to the rough nature of the splashed on signatures, which caused an increase in surface drag.

The flight was not exactly smooth for *5 GRAND* and its crew. Departing Newfoundland, the weather was fairly dismal, but the crew made the decision to press on, rather than wait a few days for possibly better conditions. However, the winds aloft were higher than forecast, and they were blowing right on the nose of the Fort – odd, since winds were usually favouring the flights to the east. Combined with the wind and the slightly decreased speed of the Fortress due to the paint work, fuel consumption was much higher than planned. As the crew spotted Ireland through a hole in the clouds, the needles on the fuel gauges were swinging towards empty, and one engine cut out as the aircraft taxied to its parking spot after a successful landing.

The arrival of the aircraft in Britain caused additional press but, oddly, Unger and his crew were transferred to another air-

ABOVE As the nose of 43-37716 comes out of the assembly jig, a worker affixes appropriate posters to the unit. Note the bare metal finish, although the cheek gun assembly (extreme left) has been sprayed in zinc chromate

craft and, after additional work at a combat depot, 5 *GRAND* was assigned to the 333rd BS/96th BG at Snetterton Heath, in Norfolk. It received the unit's large black square marking on its vertical tail, onto which was painted the code letter 'C', whilst its fuselage was adorned with the letters BXH.

Fate was not particular kind to 5 *GRAND*, for on a local flight in August 1944 (prior to its premier combat sortie) the aircraft suffered an electrical failure which meant its pilot, Lt Jack Bimemiller, could not lower the bomber's undercarriage. Having jettisoned the ball turret, the pilot was ordered to crashland at Honington, in Suffolk, which was the 3rd Bomb Division's major repair depot. The forced-landing did a fair amount of damage, ripping out the bomb bay doors and tearing up a great deal of lower fuselage skin, as well as writing off the wing flaps, engines and propellers.

Despite the damage, the USAAF felt that the aircraft was repairable, and a combat repair team went to work returning the B-17G to airworthiness in quick time. 5 *GRAND* would go on to complete a total of 78 missions with a variety of crews, its gunners also claiming two fighters destroyed.

With the war in Europe successfully completed, the now rather battered and faded 5 *GRAND* made its way back to Seattle, where it landed on 29 June 1945 for a war bond tour.

The rear fuselage is moved via overhead crane to mate with the forward section. Note that many of the 'Rosies' had hopefully added their addresses and phone numbers to their names!

LEFT Workers on the forward section of the fuselage take a few minutes from their allocated tasks to sign their names. *5 GRAND* added an almost party mood to the never-ending work of the Boeing production line as workers signed their names. Virtually every part of the aircraft was covered

BELOW As the aircraft neared completion, the vertical fin received a covering of paper explaining what the aircraft was all about, while a large '5000' was held by wires atop the fuselage. Note the cradle in the foreground containing four .50-cal Brownings and ammunition belts for installation in the bomber

Thousands of Boeing employees were able to visit the bomber, and many found that their original signatures were still in place.

At this point, local officials began making noises about preserving the bomber for the City of Seattle as a monument to its vast war effort. However, in August 1945 *5 GRAND* was flown to Lubbock, in Texas, for repair and refitting, before being placed in storage at Kingman, Arizona.

By the end of the year, work was still going on to get the bomber back to Seattle for a permanent memorial at the Seattle Historical Society. The government was apparently willing to give the aircraft to the city, but the *Seattle Star* for 3 January 1946 reported that 'city officials were a bit leery about undertaking to provide a separate building, which they said would be costly'.

No one apparently wanted to take any responsibility in the matter, and the Reconstruction Finance Corporation sold all the aircraft at Kingman (over 5400 combat types) to one scrapper, who immediately began melting down the aircraft – a process that took two years. Somewhere during that period, *5 GRAND* was chopped up and fed into the smelters.

ABOVE This magnificent in-flight view of the aircraft (the name *5 GRAND* had been added by this point) illustrates the thousands of signatures on the bomber's under surfaces. Note that the aircraft retains its early B-17E style tail gun position

BELOW This view of the Boeing ramp shows female workers preparing *5 GRAND* for its its final series of flight tests

LEFT A number of crews flew *5 GRAND* during its long tour with the 96th BG

BELOW A USAAF captain examines the bomb mission symbols on *5 GRAND*'s vertical tail during its stop at Boeing. By this time, the aircraft's code of BXH had been replaced with a single C

ABOVE On 7 February 1947, aviation historian William T Larkins begged and pleaded to be let into the vast scrapyard at Kingman, Arizona, where over 5400 combat aircraft were being reduced to aluminium ingots. A virtually complete (minus machine guns) *5 GRAND* was one of those aircraft neatly parked on the desert waste, efforts to preserve the machine having fallen through. The historic Fortress was fed into the smelters soon after this photo was taken. Fortunately, Larkins was allowed to photograph this aircraft, and numerous others, before his allotted time ran out and he had to leave the yard

RIGHT As one of the last B-17Gs built by Boeing, this aircraft was covered in bomb markers denoting all the raids carried out by the Fort up to that point in the war. The application of these must have been one hell of a job, as they cover every bombing raid ever flown by the aircraft from December 1941 (note the Lingayen Bay decal just forward of the women crouched on the tailplane) through to at least March 1945

ABOVE Aside from *5 Grand*, numerous other Forts were also adorned with morale-boosting placards usually just prior to them being rolled out. This B-17G was purchased through the sale of war bonds, hence the collection box in the foreground

CHAPTER 7

FRONTLINE

RIGHT The early days of the B-17 war in the Pacific were a period of hardship for men and machines alike. The majority of the Forts in the Philippines were destroyed in the opening days of the war, and survivors fought a rearguard action back to Australia. B-17E 41-9055 *Nippon Miss* of the 7th BG is seen being bombed up for a mission against the Japanese in New Guinea. With never more than 100 Forts in action over the Pacific at any one time, the B-17 was to gain its fame in the hostile skies over Europe

The B-17F took the war to Hitler's Germany. With escorting fighters weaving a web overhead, these perfectly formated F-models of the 390th BG ('Square J') head out on a mission

ABOVE B-17F 42-3352 *Virgin's Delight* was assigned to the 94th BG's ('Square A') 410th BS when photographed bombing the Focke-Wulf assembly plant near Marienburg on 9 October 1943.

Gen Ira Eaker called this mission 'a classic example of precision bombing', for only two B-17s were lost on the raid, and all but nine of the aircraft in the five groups despatched hit the target.

Virgin's Delight was later lost on 29 November 1943, when it crashed in the North Sea after being hit by flak over Solingen. Of the ten-man crew, just one survived to be made a PoW

LEFT B-17F 42-30230 *Homesick Angel* down in an English field on 24 August 1943. Pilot, Boardman Reed (562nd BS/388th BG) had let his co-pilot take the bomber up on a test flight to run in a new engine and the latter promptly ran the aircraft out of 'gas', resulting in this belly landing, which wrote off the bomber. Note that the wing de-icers have been removed from this aircraft, for at that time they were thought to be prone to catching fire if hit during combat. Reed gave the aircraft its name because it 'was the best climbing B-17 I had flown'

ABOVE In aerial combat, casualties were not always caused by the enemy. This B-17F, from the 94th BG ('Square A'), was hit by 500-lb bombs dropped from a Fort flying above it aircraft – indicating that one of the boxes was out of formation. The wartime press release stated that the aircraft recovered and beat all the other Forts back to base. However, eyewitness accounts state that the B-17 continued in a steepening descent into downtown Berlin, with none of the crew having been seen to have bailed out

ABOVE Boeing-built B-17F 42-30604 was photographed on 4 September 1944 at a Luftwaffe airfield between Versailles and Chateaufort, in France. This 350th BS/100th BG ('Square D') Fort, which had been named *Badger's Beauty V*, was apparently hit by flak during a raid on St Dizier and crash-landed near Caen on 4 October 1943 while under the command of Lt Harold Hellstrom – four of the crew evaded capture and six were caught and made PoWs. When discovered by advancing American troops some 11 months later, the aircraft was one of three Forts at the field. It does not appear that any effort was made to eliminate USAAF markings, and the original Army caption released with this photo states that the bombers were destroyed by retreating Germans as they fled the airfield in the face of the Allied advance

RIGHT Two 388th BG B-17Gs head out low over the ocean en route to The Netherlands on 2 May 1945. Note the chin turret and waist position .50-cal weapons have been removed. The bombers were on an emergency supply mission to drop food and supplies to Dutch civilians that had been savaged by retreating Nazis

BELOW When each and every F- and G-model Fortress left for Europe, it was fully equipped, carrying its own tool kit, manuals, wheel chocks and a set of engine and canvas flying surface covers for cold weather. It was not all that common to see the latter in place, but this shot of B-17G-15-VE 42-97522 shows the aircraft fully battened down against ice and snow during a brief stay in Gander, Newfoundland, on its way overseas during 1944. Examining the original print, someone has written in chalk 'Stay Out, CO' by the rear entrance door. This aircraft also has the three-piece canted enclosed waist gun windows installed at modification centres. The window had a flat centre panel, with the weapon in a K-5 mount. Also, this B-17G features a H_2X radar scanner unit in the position formerly occupied by the belly turret. Once in flight, the unit could be extended, and its operation was controlled by a crewman in the radio station area. This aircraft flew with both the 482nd and 305th BGs, before being salvaged on 1 May 1944

LEFT B-17G-80-BO 43-38712 *Buddy Buddy* of the 710th BS/447th BG somehow managed to return to base after having most of its nose blown off in a combat. Note how part of the upper nose has curled back over the cockpit, the left '.50-cal' is hanging from the side still in its mount and the bombardier's seat remains in position. One can not image what it must have been like attempting to fly the bomber with a hurricane wind blowing through the fuselage

BELOW B-17F *Old 66* displays an impressive number of bomb mission symbols, along with the improved cheek guns positions that were initially added at the combat modification centres, before being incorporated into the production lines

B-17G 42-31909 *NINE O NINE* has another combat mission symbol added to its tally. This aircraft achieved an Eighth Air Force record when it flew 140 missions without a single abort whilst serving with the 323rd BS/91st BG at Bassingbourn between February 1944 and VE-Day. It was scrapped at Kingman in 1946

ABOVE B-17G-65-BO 43-37565 *Songoon*, formerly of the 571st BS/390th BG, is seen at Bradley Field, Connecticut, during May 1945. One of thousands of returning combat veterans, the aircraft was scrapped at Kingman in 1946. Note how its nose turret guns have been removed and the unit turned sideways to create the least amount of drag during the transatlantic flight

LEFT Even before the war was over, Forts were being scrapped in America. Photographed by William T Larkins at Kelly Field, in Texas, during 1944, this view shows the gutted fuselage of a rare B-17D (nicknamed *The Gold Brick*) awaiting final scrapping among a few other early Forts and surplus P-40s. Most D-models had been lost in the Pacific in the first weeks of the war when the Japanese invaded the Philippines

ABOVE William T Larkins' classic photograph of over 7000 Flying Fortresses, Liberators and assorted other combat aircraft at Kingman, Arizona, on 8 February 1947. Although offered for sale, precious few of these aircraft were sold to civilian buyers, the majority being purchased by a scrapper. Within two years all had been consigned to history

CHAPTER 8

THEY FLEW FORTS

BELOW Happy to be home, the crew of *WHEEL 'N DEAL* pause for a portrait next to their Fort's number four engine, which is minus its Hamilton Standard propeller. This aircraft, B-17F 41-24511, was assigned to the 91st BG's 322nd BS, and had taken part in a daylight raid against Wilhelmshaven, during which it received heavy damage from the German defenders. Swiftly repaired, the Bassingbourn-based bomber was not so lucky next time round, for it was struck by flak during a raid to Solingen on 1 December 1943 and crashed near Düsseldorf. Nine crewmen were captured and the tenth was killed

ABOVE Waist gunners aboard a B-17E receive training prior to an overseas posting. The men were firing their .50-cal guns at targets painted on the side of a cliff as the B-17 manoeuvred in the area. They were required to wear full cold weather gear to get used to the equipment. Note the exposed overhead control cables

RIGHT *KNOCK-OUT DROPPER's* pilot, 1st Lt Malcolm Brown, shakes hands with his co-pilot, Capt George Mackin, after completing yet another combat mission

LEFT When the crews of other 100th BG B-17Gs saw this fellow aircraft limping back over France after receiving massive damage, they thought the stricken Fort was finished. However, when back at base and debriefing, the crews were astounded to see the bomber come in for a safe landing. Incredulous British guards examine the damaged B-17G at its Thorpe Abbotts base, in Norfolk. The Fort, named *Hang*

the Expense III, was flown by John Nilsson – described as 'the 100th's most prodigal pilot', he wrecked at least seven B-17s during his tour, which possibly a record! All his aircraft were named *Hang the Expense*

BELOW Everybody sent snapshots back home. This truck driver poses for a portrait with B-17G *"Lil Audrey"* of the 92nd BG at Podington, in Bedfordshire

BELOW Certainly one of the most famous Forts of the war was B-17F 41-24485 *MEMPHIS BELLE* of the 91st BG's 324th BS. With a great deal of propaganda fanfare, the military covered the aircraft's 25th combat mission in great detail, even making a feature film about the event. The USAAF listed the 'BELLE as being the first Fort to officially complete 25 combat missions, and the crew was photographed on 17 May 1943 at its Bassingbourn base. They are, from left to right: Harold Loch, top turret gunner; Cecil Scott, ball turret gunner; Robert Hanson, radio operator; Jim Verinis, co-pilot; Robert Morgan, pilot; Chuck Leighton, navigator; John Quinlan, tail gunner; Tony Nastal, right waist gunner; Vince Evans, bombardier; and Bill Winchell, left waist gunner. In 1989 their exploits were once again the subject of a feature film

OPPOSITE LEFT Airfield personnel fire a flare to start the launch of the 388th BG's B-17Gs on yet another mission to Germany. Note the rather improvised pole for the windsock!

ABOVE Enlisted personnel from the 388th BG invited some of the local lasses to their Knettishall base, in Norfolk, for an old-fashioned pig roast on their day off. Some of the guest seem less than pleased at the sight of the pig!

BELOW Another mission completed. The crew of *Old Granddad* walk away from their Fort after completing their 25th mission, during which time the aircraft's gunners were credited with nine fighters destroyed

Photographed at the Curtiss-Wright plant at Caldwell-Wright Airport in New Jersey on 13 March 1943, crew members from HELL'S ANGELS pose for a portrait. Wright, builders of the Cyclone engine, was the first stop for the B-17F on a 30-day tour of US warplants – HELL'S ANGELS had successfully completed 48 bombing missions. Front row, left to right: MSgt Fabian Folmer; Capt Irl Baldwin, pilot on 25 missions; Capt John Johnston, pilot on six missions; and SSgt Kasmer Wegrzyn. Rear, left to right: Sgt John Kosilla; TSgt Edward West Jr; and Sgt Wilson Fairfield

ABOVE Unsung groundcrew. The ground and maintenance crew of B-17F *DELTA REBEL NO. 2* service the number three engine between raids. Sgt Maurice Gole, crew chief, is examining the propeller hub. This photo was taken in the western end of the hangar used by the 323rd BS/91st BG at Bassingbourn during February 1943

RIGHT As gunners began to suffer appalling casualties from flak and fighters, various schemes were undertaken to offer increased protection. This rather odd photograph, taken during February 1944, shows Pvt Lee Morris wearing body armour while Pfc Kenneth Tracy wears a vintage suit of armour. The body armour was being shown publicly for the first time at the Army Ordnance Exhibit in the Chrysler Building in New York

ABOVE A USAAF ferry crew prepares to take fly a brand new B-17G from Seattle to a USAAF modification centre

OPPOSITE RIGHT 'He knows a rat when he sees one', stated the opening line of the caption for this photograph, taken during March 1943 at Harlingen, Texas – one of the larger air gunnery training bases. Sgt James Gamble, completing his training before being assigned to a Fort bomb group, was a rat exterminator for eight years before joining the USAAF. He is seen with his 'rat mascot' that he ha made during his spare time in Texas

LEFT Maj Boardman C Reed, squadron commander of the 562nd BS/388th BG, pauses for a portrait by his Fortress at Knettishell (AAF Station 136)

BELOW Members of the 388th BG gather for a '200 mission party' and ball game again at Knettishall. The fabulous array of A-2 jacket art on display is noteworthy

RIGHT Maj Edward Sustrick, left, and Sgt William Lyon wear M3 and M4 helmets respectively. The M3, developed by the Ordnance Department for the USAAF, could be worn by most members of a B-17 crew. It was of one-piece construction, with hinged flaps. The M4 was specially developed for use by gunners who had limited space in their turrets. This official photograph was taken during January 1943

BELOW It wasn't easy in the ETO – the body of a waist gun-ner is removed from a B-17 upon its return to base. Note the red surround to the national insignia

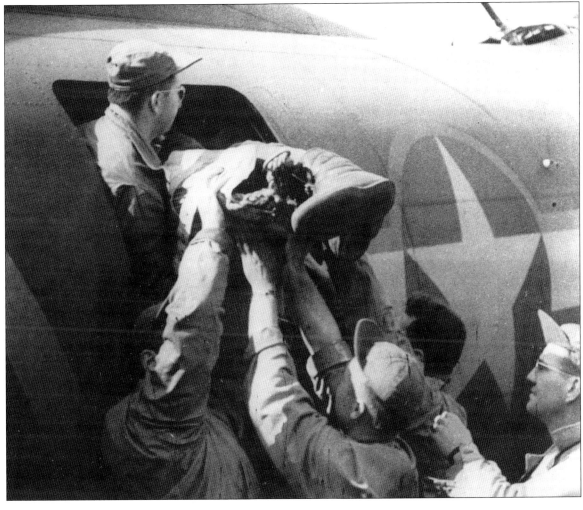

LEFT Crew members of B-17G *Flag Ship* examine their aircraft, which carried the first American flag to fly over Berlin in the first American daylight raid on the German capital

BELOW The route home – 50 B-17s landed at fields between Springfield and Hartford, Connecticut, in April 1945 to mark the first flight of a mass aerial ferry service from England to America, which was expected to return more than 40,000 Eighth Air Force personnel home. At Bradley Field, Cpl Samuel De Leo, Flt Off Robert Adams, SSgt Steve Melnick and Pfc Robert Spence examine a map of the route they had just flown

ABOVE Popular 1938 film *Test Pilot* had starred Clark Gable, Myrna Loy and virtually the entire complement of the 20th BS's YIB-17s – one of which is seen in the background of this scene shot at March Field. Little did Gable know at the time, but the next few years would see the actor forging a close association with Boeing's much-improved Flying Fortress

LEFT When Gable's wife Carole Lombard was killed in the mysterious crash of a TWA DC-3 during early 1942 while returning from a successful war bond tour, the devastated actor attempted to join the military. However, President Roosevelt stated he was needed at home, where he could use his talents in films useful for the war effort. Gable, however, eventually got his way, and is seen here being sworn into the military by Col Malcolm Andruss

LEFT At age 41, Gable went to Officer Candidate School in Miami, and following graduation was ordered by Gen 'Hap' Arnold to star in a film about aerial gunners. Accordingly, Gable went to several gunnery schools before reporting overseas for assignment with the 351st BG, with the directive to 'making a film showing the day-to-day activities of a typical heavy bombardment group'. The movie would have special emphasis placed on the gunners. Based at Polebrook, Gable flew five combat missions with the 351st, and he is seen here with the group's famous B-17F *DELTA REBEL NO. 2*

ABOVE Even after the war, Clark Gable's association with the B-17 would continue with the popular 1948 film *Command Decision*. This realistic set shows him plotting a B-17 raid deep into Germany

APPENDICES

FLYING FORTRESS SPECIFICATIONS

MODEL 299

Span	103 ft 9$^3/_8$ in
Length	68 ft 9 in
Height	14 ft 11$^{15}/_{16}$ in
Wing Area	1420 sq ft
Empty Weight	21,657 lb
Gross Weight	32,432 lb
Max Weight	38,055 lb
Max Speed	236 mph
Cruise Speed	140 mph
Ceiling	24,600 ft
Range	3100 miles
Powerplants	Pratt & Whitney S1EG Hornet/750 hp

Y1B-17

Span	103 ft 9$^3/_8$ in
Length	68 ft 4 in
Height	18 ft 4 in
Wing Area	1420 sq ft
Empty Weight	24,460 lb
Gross Weight	34,800 lb
Max Weight	42,600 lb
Max Speed	255 mph
Cruise Speed	217 mph
Ceiling	30,500 ft
Climb	10,000 ft in 6.5 min
Range	1400 miles
Powerplants	Wright R-1820-39/1000 hp

B-17B

Span	103 ft 9$^3/_8$ in
Length	67 ft 9 in
Height	18 ft 4 in
Wing Area	1420 sq ft
Empty Weight	27,652 lb
Gross Weight	37,997 lb
Max Weight	46,178 lb
Range	1250 miles
Ceiling	30,000 ft
Max Speed	292 mph
Cruise Speed	225 mph
Powerplants	Wright R-1820-51/1200 hp

B-17C

Span	103 ft 9$^3/_4$ in
Length	67 ft 9 in
Height	18 ft 4 ft
Wing Area	1420 sq ft
Max Speed	323 mph at 25,000 ft
Range	2400 miles
Empty Weight	29,025 lb
Gross Weight	47,242 lb
Powerplants	Wright R-1820-65/1000 hp at 25,000 ft

B-17E

Span	103 ft 9$^3/_4$ in
Length	73 ft 10 in
Height	19 ft 2 in
Wing Area	1420 sq ft
Empty Weight	32,250 lb
Gross Weight	40,260 lb
Max Weight	53,000 lb
Max Speed	317 mph at 25,000 ft
Cruise Speed	195 mph
Landing Speed	80 mph
Ceiling	36,000 ft
Range	2000 miles
Powerplants	Wright R-1820-64/1200 hp at 25,000 ft

B-17F

Span	103 ft 9³/₄ in
Length	74 ft 9 in
Height	19 ft 1 in
Wing Area	1420 sq ft
Empty Weight	34,000 lb
Gross Weight	55,000 lb
Max Weight	65,500 lb
Max Speed	299 mph at 25,000 ft
Cruise Speed	200 mph
Landing Speed	90 mph
Ceiling	37,500 ft
Range	1300 miles
Powerplants	Wright R-1820-97/1380 hp (war emergency only)

B-17G

Span	103 ft 9³/₄ in
Length	74 ft 4 in
Height	19 ft 1 in
Wing Area	1420 sq ft
Empty Weight	36,120 lb
Gross Weight	55,000 lb
Max Weight	65,500 lb
Max Speed	287 mph at 25,000 ft
Cruise Speed	182 mph
Landing Speed	90 mph
Ceiling	35,600 ft
Range	2000 miles
Powerplants	Wright R-1820-97/1380 hp (war emergency only)

XB-40

Span	103 ft 9³/₄ in
Length	74 ft 9 in
Height	19 ft 1 in
Wing Area	1420 sq ft
Empty Weight	38,235 lb
Loaded Weight	58,000 lb
Max Weight	63,300 lb
Wing Loading	40.8 lb/sq ft
Power Loading	12.1 lb/hp
Max Speed	292 mph at 25,000 ft
Cruise Speed	192 mph
Climb	20,000 ft in 48.1 min
Ceiling	25,000 ft
Range	2250 miles
Powerplants	Wright R-1820-97/1380 hp (war emergency only)

XB-38

Span	103 ft 9³/₄ in
Length	74 ft 9 in
Height	19 ft 2 in
Wing Area	1420 sq ft
Empty Weight	34,700 lb
Loaded Weight	56,000 lb
Max Weight	64,000 lb
Wing Loading	39.4 lb/sq in
Power Loading	9.8 lb/hp
Max Speed	327 mph at 25,000 ft
Cruise Speed	226 mph
Ceiling	29,600 ft
Powerplants	Allison V-1710-89/1425 hp

FLYING FORTRESS SERIALS

Model 299	c/n 1963/X13372
Y1B-17	36-149 to -161
	(c/n 1973 to 1985)
Y1B-17A	37-369
	(c/n 1987)
B-17B	38-211 to -223, 38-258 to -270,
	38-583/-584, -610 and 39-1 to -10
	(c/n 2004 to 2042)
B-17C	40-2042 to -2079
	(c/n 2043 to 2080)
B-17D	40-3059 to -3100
	(c/n 2087 to 2128)
B-17E	41-2393 to -2669 and 41-9011 to
	-9245
	(c/n 2204 to 2480 and 2483 to 2717)
B-17F(Boeing)	41-24340 to -24639, 42-5050 to
	-5484 and 42-29467 to -31031
	(c/n 3025 to 3324, 3589 to 4023
	and 4581 to 6145)
B-17F(Douglas)	42-2964 to -3562, 42-33714/-33715
	and 42-33717 to -37220
	(c/n 7900 to 8498, 8500/8501
	and 8503 to 8506)
B-17F(Vega)	42-5705 to -6204
	(c/n 6001 to 6500)
B-17G(Boeing)	42-31032 to -32116, 42-97058 to
	-97407, 42-102379 to -102978 and
	43-37509 to -39508
	(c/n 6146 to 7230, 7531 to 7880,
	7881 to 8480 and 8487 to 10486)
B-17G(Douglas)	42-3483 to -3563, 42-37714 to
	38213, 42-106984 to -107233,
	44-6001 to -7000 and 44-83236
	to -83885
	(c/n 8419 to 8499, 8500 to 8999,
	21899 to 22148, 22224 to 23223
	and 31877 to 32526)
B-17G(Vega)	42-39758 to 40057, 42-97436 to
	-98035, 44-8001 to -9000 and
	44-85492 to -85841
	(c/n 6501 to 6800, 6801 to 7400,
	7401 to 8400 and 8401 to 8750)
XB-38	41-2401
XB-40	41-24341
YB-40	42-5732 to 5744 and 5871, 5920,
	5921 and 5923 to 5925
TB-40	42-5833/4834, 5872 and 5926

ROYAL AIR FORCE FLYING FORTRESSES

FORTRESS I

RAF Serial	C/N	USAAC Serial
AN518	2044	40-2043
AN519	2045	40-2044
AN520	2052	40-2051
AN521	2053	40-2052
AN522	2054	40-2053
AN523	2056	40-2055
AN524	2057	40-2056
AN525	2058	40-2057
AN526	2061	40-2060
AN527	2062	40-2061
AN528	2065	40-2064
AN529	2066	40-2065
AN530	2067	40-2066
AN531	2069	40-2068
AN532	2070	40-2069
AN533	2072	40-2071
AN534	2074	40-2073
AN535	2076	40-2075
AN536	2077	40-2076
AN537	2080	40-2079

FORTRESS II (B-17F)
FA695 and FA713

FORTRESS IIA (B-17E)
FK184 to FK213, FG449 to FG460 and FG 462 to FG464

FORTRESS III (B-17G)
HB761 to HB 790 (Boeing), HB791 to HB793, HB795 and HB796, HB799 to HB803, HB805, HB815 to HB820, KH998 and KH999, KJ100 to KJ127 and KL830 to KL837 (Vega)

EIGHTH AIR FORCE B-17 UNIT SYMBOLS

91st BG	Triangle A
92nd BG	Triangle B
303rd BG	Triangle C
305th BG	Triangle G
306th BG	Triangle H
351st BG	Triangle J
379th BG	Triangle K
381st BG	Triangle L
384th BG	Triangle P
401st BG	Triangle S
457th BG	Triangle U
398th BG	Triangle W
94th BG	Square A
95th BG	Square B
96th BG	Square C
100th BG	Square D
388th BG	Square H
390th BG	Square J
447th BG	Square K
452nd BG	Square L
487th BG	Square P
486th BG	Square W
34th BG	A
385th BG	E
490th BG	L
493rd BG	T

EIGHTH AIR FORCE B-17 SQUADRON CODES

337th BS	AW	532nd BS	VE
334th BS	BG	358th BS	VK
568th BS	BI	533rd BS	VP
546th BS	BK	524th BS	WA
359th BS	BN	364th BS	WF
368th BS	BO	369th BS	WW
338th BS	BX	365th BS	XK
569th BS	CC	332nd BS	XM
324th BS	DF	349th BS	XR
570th BS	DI	508th BS	YB
511th BS	DS	838th BS	2C
351th BS	EP	837th BS	4F
336th BS	ET	836th BS	2G
571th BS	FC	835th BS	H8
527th BS	FO	602nd BS	K8
525th BS	FR	833rd BS	4N
534th BS	GD	603rd BS	N7
410th BS	GL	600th BS	N8
427th BS	GN	601st BS	3O
367th BS	GY	8th TO	Q3
613th BS	IN	832nd BS	3R
614th BS	IW	36th BS	R4
615th BS	IY	839th BS	R5
545th BS	JD	834th BS	2S
422nd BS	JJ		
326th BS	JW		
366th BS	KY		
418th BS	LD		
526th BS	LF		
322nd BS	LG		
401st BS	LL		
350th BS	LN		
812th BS	MI		
535th BS	MS		
413th BS	MZ		
325th BS	NV		
335th BS	OE		
323rd BS	OR		
813th BS	PC		
360th BS	PU		
407th BS	PY		
331th BS	QE		
339th BS	QJ		
412th BS	QW		
423rd BS	RD		
509th BS	RQ		
612th BS	SC		
814th BS	SI		
547th BS	SO		
544th BS	SU		
333rd BS	TS		
510th BS	TU		
327th BS	UX		

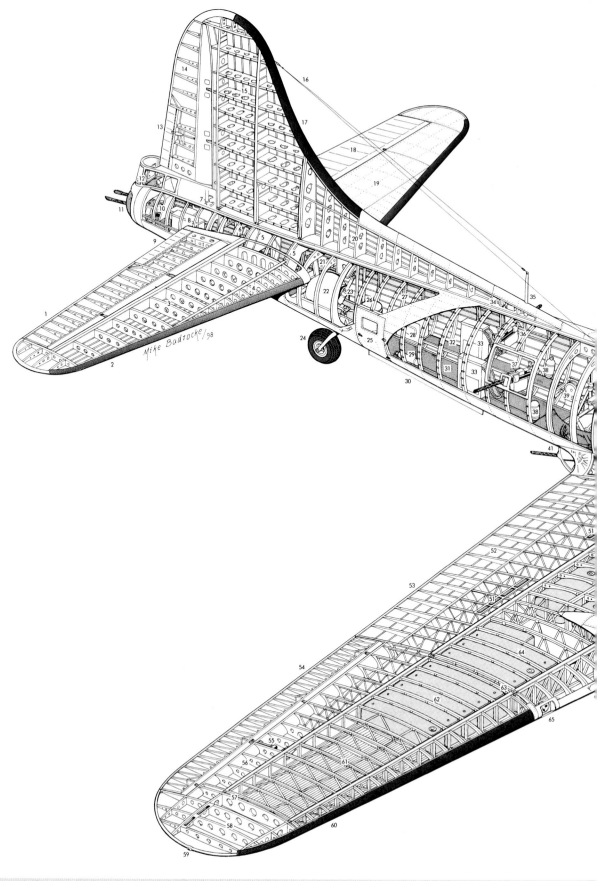

Mike Badrocke/98